WHISPERS OF *Love*

A Journey to Self-Love
Through the Guidance of Animals and Spirit

KELLY RENEE VIZZINI

Whispers of Love
A Journey to Self-Love Through the Guidance of Animals and Spirit

Book Design by
Transcendent Publishing
Author's Photos by Alayne Vogel/Memory Layne Photography

ISBN: 979-8-9900956-0-1

Printed in the United States of America.

To my mom,
all the animal beings, and
to those walking this journey with me in Spirit — with deep
gratitude for your love, guidance, and infinite support.
To my editor who helped me dig through the webbing
of my words, and to you, the reader, may you find a
piece of yourself in these pages.
Thank you.

TABLE OF CONTENTS

Acknowledgments vii

Introduction: A Prescription of Love ix

PART I: The Journey to Integrate the Dark and Light . . 1

Chapter 1: When Early Stories Release, the Lessons and
        Love Appear 3

Chapter 2: The Faces of Expansion 9

Chapter 3: Re-Connection with Nature Brings
        Opportunities for Expansion 19

Chapter 4: A Leap of Faith 23

Chapter 5: Walking With Change From Within 29

Chapter 6: Big Changes On The Horizon 35

Chapter 7: A Generation Ends 39

Chapter 8: Venturing into the Unknown 41

Chapter 9: The Heart Opens 45

PART II: Love Finds A Door **51**

Chapter 10: An Intuitive Idea Sparks Action. 53

Chapter 11: School's In Session 59

Chapter 12: No Two Respond the Same 77

Chapter 13: Connections and Synchronicity. 87

Chapter 14: The Rise and Fall of the Water 95

Chapter 15: Lessons in Listening. 107

Chapter 16: The Power of Love 117

Chapter 17: The Caregiver: Being Seen Where They Are . 125

Chapter 18: Being Seen 135

Chapter 19 : The Look of Respect 151

Chapter 20: A Walk Of Love. 155

Chapter 21: The Last Climb 167

Chapter 22: Learning To Hear My Own Voice. 173

Chapter 23: Putting The Puzzle Pieces Together 179

Chapter 24: Integrating and Embodying the Teachings . 189

Chapter 25: The Walk of Healing 195

Continue The Journey 201

About the Author 203

ACKNOWLEDGMENTS

*T*he real names of the animal beings and people have not been used, as it is my belief that *all beings,* especially those in animal form, feel the energy of those ingesting the teachings within this book's pages. They all know it has been written and with their approval.

The lessons and love shared here are done so with my deepest respect for and trust in these beautiful relationships, to the best of my knowledge at the time and space when experiences occurred and while writing this book.

Thank you for believing in me, working with me on the journey to be a voice for you, myself, and all the amazing gifts of connection. May love and blessings always support you, both on this side and across the Rainbow Bridge.

With love and light,
Kelly Renee Vizzini

A PRESCRIPTION OF LOVE

*H*ave you ever wondered what the journey of healing may look like? Where the adventure will take you? Or what steps may come across your path to get you there? We think of healing as doctors' appointments and prescriptions of medicine, often in combination with nutrition and exercises to increase mobility and fitness.

However, we often discover, sometimes years later, that we have been working to heal on the subconscious level, through our thoughts, choices, and actions. These ingredients for my own unique recipe or prescription for healing, appeared one by one in my life – rarely recognized or understood in the moment as such, yet transformative in many unique and great ways. The "prescription" was the pieces I was drawn or guided to amongst the details of whatever situation, relationship, or experience was happening at the time. Ultimately, they revealed themselves to be part of a jigsaw puzzle I didn't even know I was solving; they also encompassed *more of my lifetime than I realized as things shifted, the murkiness cleared, and the bigger, higher picture took shape.*

Healing isn't a one-size-fits-all (or even a one-size-fits-most) journey, but an individualized work of art we create as we take a deep dive beneath the surface of life into the emotions and experiences we have held at the depths of our being. It is uncovering the hidden treasure in the locked rooms of our subconscious minds, our inner hearts, and the voices of our own bodies.

Many of us do not know when the steps began to unfold or the threads unraveled like a giant yarn ball from the heavens, the sky, or the Great Beyond. For what appeared, whether in shiny or rough form, led us through the ethers of time and space to the mechanism of healing. They were footsteps moving forward, yet often appearing backward or circling in a cluster of confusion. Yes, even then, active healing was in play.

We review the timeframes, scenarios, and memories to identify a connecting point to where our dis-ease, illness, or imbalance began. What were we doing, seeing, or hearing? What were we feeling? We begin excavating our personal history, following the trail of our emotions, perspectives, and the way we responded or reacted to life. This becomes an unfolding in our immediate world as we see the roles friends, family, teachers, peers, colleagues, bosses, and Spirit have played on our stage. Some have main parts and others have minor ones, yet each is significant to the plot.

This theater production depicts how our choices have maneuvered the pendulum back and forth. We see how our thoughts and beliefs have led us to ignore the self's needs and its voice yelling to be heard as the focus shifts to the needs of others in the room, on the phone, or over the email. Our connection to that inner voice begins to fade because we have failed once again to heed the call of the one with whom we are most linked, the one with whom we were born, and the one with whom we will die to honor another's deeds. We are once again muffling or drowning out the one who is us, and it is this relationship we must mend to heal our mind, body, and/or soul and bring harmony to our heart.

Where did we lose ourselves? At what point did we begin choosing not to listen? At what age did we begin drowning or stuffing our emotions so we didn't have to hear our inner critic punishing us for not being good enough, saying people would not accept who we are? When did we start talking to ourselves with disdain instead of self-love? Why did we often feel the energy of what people weren't saying, while the one thing we wanted most seemed out of reach with all but a select few?

We searched for acceptance, all the while unaware that we had to give it to ourselves first. We looked for love outside us, not understanding we had to love ourselves – both the light and shadow. We did not know that to truly love another we must love the one within us – to care for her, hear her, believe and trust in her, and to allow her voice to be heard and her light to be seen.

Sometimes we wonder what brought disorder or imbalance to our doorstep once again – be it in the form of a friendship, lover, family, or acquaintance. To find the answer, we must step back far enough to remember that we are all mirrors or projections of one another; rarely do we see in another what is not within us in some way, shape, or form. Most often that most frustrating element is in an aspect we choose not to see, one long ago hidden within our shadow. It can be minor – one that we show only to ourselves, or one we show to others for their own lessons. Knowing that we hold the key to releasing the pattern is not always readily understood, and the guidance we receive by going within is not comprehended during the initial phase. To unearth the answer or greater aware-ness, we must do some digging – and then choose to either acknowl-edge and accept or acknowledge and change that part of us that has hidden in the dark for way too long. Then, we can take her by the hand and fully integrate to be one with who we are.

Just like our organs hold emotions, so do our shadows. Dis-covering the situation, thought, or experience at the core of a shadow is most often depicted through our strongest emotions or the areas of emptiness that appear when we are exhausted after an unusually taxing life phase. It can also trigger us to respond with unhealthy habits such as poor eating, negative thought pat-terns, and the like, not recognizing that in order to heal we had to soothe ourselves or plug the energy drain that left us empty, hollow, and in a funk.

Yes, healing will take you to places, new and old, that you didn't want to travel to, as well as an invisible list of tasks, steps, or bucket list items that had to be brought into the light. Like a desert tortoise that carries the world upon its back, so too have you carried emotions, struggles, and unspoken words. Releasing them is necessary for lightening and healing the body – and breaking the patterns that keep us calling in what we know we don't want.

Throughout our lives, there are many opportunities and expe-riences that, though very different, bring us to a similar space. There is also a range of experiences that occur in relationships of all types – including, and most importantly, our relationship with ourselves via our thoughts, emotions, actions, and beliefs. Yes, how we learn to treat our own self can be the golden key to unlocking the patterns, both desirable and undesirable, in our life.

If you are like me, you grew up in an era when understanding the need for self-care was often confused with selfishness. This is especially true for girls, for we were the caretakers of everyone – both those who supported us and those who hurt us, be it physically, emotionally, or verbally (in the latter case often using humor as a cover). It isn't until many decades later that we realize how blind we have been to the needs of our bodies and souls, for they were buried beneath layers of perceptions and illusions of what we had been taught love was.

Much of my understanding came through the unraveling process of walking away from a relationship – and seeing where similar mental and outward-facing challenges and traits had shown up elsewhere in my life. Indeed, there were several relationships carrying the same patterns that my fifty-four-year-old self felt had to stop, once and for all. This would allow me to heal by acknowledging the elements of myself that may have played a role; after all, it was my response to the wounds the other was projecting. In most cases, this is an unknown aspect on the other person's part – a role they came to play on a soul level. Yet there is a different feeling when you know in your heart that they were aware of what they were doing (i.e., through manipulation). And again, most will not own up to that – something we each must learn to accept and move beyond, as well as our own perceptions of the situation.

For me, it has been about learning the big-picture lessons that led to another experience, then integrating those lessons with an understanding of my response, or willingness to stay in the rela-tionship despite red flags. I began to look deep beneath the surface of why I have struggled to voice my observations, frustrations, and perceptions in these unhealthy relationships. Why did I hide my emotions or the vulnerable side behind a tough outer shell? What held my voice in, or what permitted the other to once again not accept my truth in the words I struggled to speak?

We must also understand the importance of self-forgiveness, and forgiveness in general, to reach the next layer of healing. And, yes, even saying the words aloud in an empty room or typing them in a text or letter never to be sent, opens the door for forgiveness and healing. Saying the words aloud or to the other within the relationship doesn't mean that it will mend, nor is it always meant to. It does not mean the individual is ready to listen, nor does it mean that they have worked on themselves in the time away. What it does mean is that I have peeled back several layers – and the way in which I respond or react to any response they may deliver determines the level of healing work that has been accomplished in the time that passed.

It is the awareness of what I am noticing, what I am feeling, and where there may still be some triggering, that informs where my inner work has taken me thus far. Yes, it was the answers to these questions that I never thought to ask myself or dig beneath the surface for – and, yet, if not for the inner work and this piv-otal relationship, I may have continued walking an unhealthy path. Understanding the lessons takes me on an even deeper dive into this relationship and others with similar undertones and threads, along with the most challenging aspects of myself and the stories that were hardest to let go of. When we dig into the stories from a higher vantage point, we are able to gain the treasure found in flipping or reframing the lesson of the story. Then we can answer the questions: What did we gain from it? What did we learn about ourselves in the experiences? For each relationship is a pattern of the choices we make in response to the choices of the other person or entity – as well as our own history. Energy also plays a huge part in the way we connect with another. It helps us determine whether it is a relationship that feels supportive on multiple levels or is solely filled with one party trying to upstage the other's experiences, making it increasingly difficult to connect and feel heard.

Another layer to this journey involves learning whether an ancestral component, one that predates our current life, is at play. This means the lesson has been handed down through the generations, with each individual getting as far as they could to find resolution or acceptance before passing along the core piece to their descendants. For example, an element of my own personality was revealed as an ancestral pattern through a conversation with crossed-over loved ones during one of my hikes. This pattern was that of a strong, silent type of personality that was often perceived to be less-than by others, as they were less likely to voice certain things. For me, this characteristic manifested as a struggle to inter-pret feelings and emotions in a way that clearly conveyed to others what I wanted to communicate.

Those who find it difficult to articulate their thoughts or feel-ings quickly, for example during a brief lull in conversation, often feel bulldozed or blocked by highly verbal people. This challenge is more pronounced with others who seem not to pause for breath, especially if you are someone who tends to follow "the rules" and feels uncomfortable interrupting to get a word in, be it with family, friends, or others. In my relationships, this misunderstanding often became an ongoing struggle for airtime, and, eventually, the "silent type" within me said less and less, rather than continuously feeling like I had to fight to get a word in. And, if we cannot be heard amongst friends and family, where else could we be?

These highly emotional components that needed to be shared were what made us the strong silent types who were repeatedly shut down or silenced by others. To stay felt like a form of settling; also, we, the silent ones, did not see ourselves as worthy of being seen and respected within these relationships – and to stay meant we were condoning that treatment. A higher awareness manifested during the writing of this that, once again showed, the outer environment was following my own inner compass.

Do all of these relationships have to end? No. Some people are able to work through these complex templates together, and, in many of my prior relationships, that was the case... from a distance. For others, for whom the concept of distance was not well received, the understanding of time away was a necessary component akin to a silent month-long journey into nature or however long it took for the mind to quiet, the constant replay of what we saw, felt, thought, or heard spoken to diminish. Time away, whether for a short period or an indefinite one, can be necessary as it takes time to recognize that we need to heal ourselves – be it through therapy, classes that give us new insight, or working with nature as our therapist, using movement, meditation, and centering through its silence and sounds that open our heart for connection, listening, and processing.

Sometimes the biggest hurdle is our inability to imagine what a wholesome relationship would look like, as we haven't been able to completely share who we are at the core or haven't felt received by the other at key moments. The more we work to break free from the silence to become a healthier version of ourselves, the more we feel the pushback to remain who the other has deemed us to be. As a result, not only is alignment within the relationship changing, but a level of toxicity can surface because remaining connected now feels unhealthy. As we shift we are, in many ways, becoming a completely new person – and learning to fully accept ourselves, perhaps for the first time ever. This in-depth exploration and journey can take moments, days, weeks, and years, for we are learning to hear the subtle voice in our body, soul, and emotions. I did much of this in nature, which became my healing place – a space for me to tune into my intuition and give myself permission to listen and understand what was being shared in that innermost sanctum of the true me.

Healing on this level through evaluation of thoughts, emotions, actions, and even non-action takes diligence, determination, and courage to follow through on what is surfacing – and determining the next piece in the puzzle. It isn't an easy or straightforward path, but one with many twists and turns. After many years of these patterns playing out in various experiences, we still may wonder what brought us to the point, finally, of saying, "No more," and instead taking what we perceive as an integral step toward change. For me, it meant understanding that what was my next best step may not be what the other person in the relationship (or a person outside the situation) would perceive as such.

If you've ever heard, "Why do you always have to do it the hard way?" know that you are not alone – and that the question itself comes from the subjective perception of the person asking it. Only someone living within my body, living in my emotions, can truly understand the choices that show up in my reality. What may seem like the clearest path to me may appear muddy to another. Often it is a question of what is innate to us and the lifetime skillset that has been the go-to. Even if you choose to work with a teacher, do not expect them to just hand you the information; we are there to learn for ourselves. Indeed, it may be the work I began with the first Reiki level, followed by the second and master levels as well as other classes and situations, that allowed me to become an observer of my own self and begin opening this doorway.

My work with those who have found their way to me and through my pet companion business has helped me learn about unconditional love from some of the gentlest and often misunderstood beings. These pets and/or companion animals in their many forms, as well as the wild living souls I encountered at parks and in the natural world, have opened the door for me to allow others into my innermost sacred way of being. My path to healing may seem unconventional to some, but rarely do we fully understand what we need in our own journey, or how calling in connection with animal beings can be part of a prescription for love and relearning to communicate.

My education was masked by the need to assist these animal beings physically, emotionally, and mentally. We have learned a lot together. "Broken" through perceived barriers, we walked the gamut of age, health, and personality to support each other on our respective paths – a process I have expanded while experiencing ways to connect, communicate, and overcome my own hurdles of insecurity, grief, and sadness to uncover the need to become aware of myself on all levels — physically, spiritually, and emotionally. Knowing how my physical vessel was feeling was not always a given through sensing alone, which speaks to just how long it had been since I'd truly heard my body talking with me.

These animals began sharing their insights with me through a paw or attention to an area of my body, such as a tight calf I hadn't recognized until the animal being drank some water and licked the location. Then I would silently ask the question, "Why is she concentrating on that?" only to discover that it hurt when I touched it. The larger picture brought through was that I wasn't taking in enough water and that my calves and legs needed some stretching. This, after two years of plantar fasciitis in both feet that I eventually relieved with stretching exercises, a massage technique with cupping moved up and down the legs, and more water intake. I also began to stretch more, both with the dogs before our walks and when I headed out for hikes.

They have taught me to celebrate the littlest to the greatest of achievements and to rediscover how to play while living life and walking through the lessons I came here at this time to learn. It is only in reflecting on these relationships over the past eight years that I have found additional meaning in many of my encounters and their teachings. I had spent years not recognizing my own body's language, sensitivity, or my energy level at any given moment; therefore, I was unable to distinguish between myself and what I was picking up from others. In fact, when I started my business, I was beginning to learn how one could actually receive body sensations such as aches and stiffness, as well as emotions, thoughts, and *the like from other people. At that point it was random – I would feel it only occasionally and discerned it even less often than that. In fact, this was not a concrete or embodied perception until the letters combined to form words on the pages of this book. I did not comprehend just how much of what I was experiencing **was not mine**. These are some of the teachings of the pets, for they are the masters of this discipline!*

You might wonder what this has to do with your pets or animal companions, and I will tell you: everything. I hope by the conclusion of this book you will have come to understand the love, lessons, and support these beautiful beings impart to us through their patient teachings, and the symbiotic relationship we achieve when we open to oneness with those who are much more like us than we perceive. The magnitude of these relationships can be just as great, rewarding, and healing as the various long- or short-term relationships we have experienced with our human friends, family members, colleagues, and so on. We can have an emotional connection with the animal beings in our lives, regardless of how frequently we see them. The depth of relationship depends on the individuals involved and what they came here to learn and teach one another – regardless of their species.

PART 1

The Journey to Integrate the Dark and Light

This first section is about taking the steps to move beneath the surface of the stories from the earlier part of my life – and grasp the morsels of love and the deeper lessons held within to assist my growth and understanding of the hidden gifts.

Chapter One

WHEN EARLY STORIES RELEASE, THE LESSONS AND LOVE APPEAR

When I first sat down to write this book, I found that what surfaced and wanted to be released onto the pages were the stories – my earliest experiences that held some deep emotional links which kept them close by, like the tools of my existence. As I reviewed those words during the first edit, my understanding of those stories and experiences began to shift. I had to take a step back and allow myself to journey within the pages. Over the next two weeks I took a deep dive into internal memories and external connections to dates and animal beings and, in that process, more fully accepting myself, my role, my actions, and my words. I discovered that the stories were now opening a new pathway within my heart, making way for the lessons and the love from within to appear, be heard and integrated.

New information, new understandings, and new processes are taking place simultaneously within me that result in my becoming a new, more embodied version of myself. This version is one able to release the hold and power that these stories had over me and receive the gift from my body and from Spirit as to what these were about. What you are reading here today is the result of that infinite love.

Questions related to an incident that occurred when I was six months old would determine some of the pathways I chose to take as I moved through my earliest years on planet Earth. We often wonder about events that bring about the learning of who we are or how we will relate and communicate in the world. We also wonder what came first, the chicken or the egg, and this too would be something I explored in much later years.

My chicken-and-egg story included a fall down a flight of cellar steps and new, unrecognized ways of communicating that brought about unconsciously learning to silence my own voice, feelings, and knowing. This led to my not knowing how to take the leap from silence to taking part in discussions – and thus allowing someone else's voice to take center stage. By-products of the fall included misalignments with the spoken words, often manifesting as challenges with recalling things that were said just moments earlier. As you can imagine, these challenges often surfaced in discussions in the classroom, social settings, or around the family dining table.

New experiences with signs, feelings, and intuitive know-ings started to surface first with the animal beings, with nature, and even through dreams. At the age of three, I went on a trip with an aunt, uncle, and their dog who we (my brother and I) viewed as a kid with lots of hair. (She even came with her own suitcase filled with toys, brushes, and goodies!) On this trip from Pennsylvania to Chicago and back, the dog and I rode in the back seat together. Looking back, I realize I was sensing that she had to go to the bathroom, and since neither of us knew how to communicate that feeling into words, I crawled onto my uncle's lap as he was driving and – to his utter dismay – peed on him. What happened next was not only humorous, but evidence of the telepathic communication between me and the dog – she crawled into his lap and did the same! This is my first memory of having a need and not understanding how to give voice to it – a pattern that would show up throughout my life in new and different ways.

Later, while staying within a couple of miles of the Chicago airport with its continuous, loud noises from planes landing close by, I desperately covered my sensitive ears and cried out in pain (whether the dog's or mine alone, I wasn't entirely sure). On the return trip, I got sick, though I don't know if it was due to the noise pollution I could not tune out or from a common cold. Whatever the cause, I was refusing to eat, and my worried aunt and uncle stopped at a local restaurant and ordered a pizza, hoping that would entice me. It didn't work, so my aunt ate a few pieces and my uncle, the majority. My next memory is of being seated between an ambulance driver and my aunt as the vehicle raced to the hospital in the middle of the night. She was filling out paperwork, and my uncle was lying in the back – both had food poisoning, but apparently his case was worse. When we got there, I sat with my aunt in a curtained-off area in the emergency room filled with bright light while my uncle got his stomach pumped.

This trip created an unknown baseline for intuitive messages coming from a variety of silent sources. Today the question is, *Did my fall as a baby bring to the surface gifts of intuitive connection, understanding, and hearing for animal beings and others perceived as silent? Or, would they have eventually manifested anyway?*

Verbal communication was not my go-to; therefore, when adults asked me questions and I did not know how to respond, my brother, who is two years older than me and *loved* to speak, would automatically answer for me. Although this was a great help at the time, it did not teach me about accessing the voice hidden within, nor did it prepare me to deal with these experiences when he wasn't around, especially in later years.

Around the age of five, I began having vivid dreams with confusing symbols, visuals, and the like. They scared me so badly that I would flee my room and take refuge on the living room couch to calm down and release the frightening images. It was there that I discovered a unique and comforting relationship with a large white birch tree that stood in our front yard just beyond the living room windows. That tree became a teacher of sorts that taught the subtle art of calming through presence with her. These experiences and dreams were kept hidden from everyone in my outside world. And yes, even at this young age I knew that nature provided a supportive place for me to recover and find peace.

A little while later, as I entered the first grade, I developed a pattern of numbing and escapism – the result of my not understanding the messages of my body on physical and emotional levels. This continued through nine years of various challenges with my teeth because I didn't know how to break through to the surface and communicate emotional responses and questions of safety; for example, when I experienced heightened sensitivity due to a natural disaster or simply feeling structures moving during a thunderstorm.

My body pushed for a manner to release all the emotions from these experiences and to change old ways of holding them in – including through the onset of menstruation at the age of nine. When I shared this with my friends, I found that my news, and changes in my physical appearance, opened a door to name-calling (I was told I was a liar) and abandoned by many. I began looking for spaces of acceptance, finding it solely within the recesses of my own mind as I used my powers of visualization to create a safe place to be myself, to feel, and play out the hormonal thoughts and emotions surfacing in my body. This was also a place to act out romantic relationships, as I felt alienated in my walk in the "real world" and knew enough, even at this young age, to know dating would not be safe.

The feeling of isolation shifted somewhat as I left elementary school behind and entered junior high. Other students were learning about puberty via a presentation while I was now in the fourth year of applied learnings – and still feeling like I was on a different path, having to work through the gap in emotional, physical, and mental maturity they naturally grew into. By this point, I had in various ways learned to turn my back on many of the traditional female attributes of nurturing self, intuition, and developing a need for deeper relationships with peers. I felt out of alignment with them to a large extent and mainly spent my time with a few close friends and family.

Television shows like *Flipper* offered advanced insight into the hidden beliefs of what I knew to be possible, and I would watch the reruns knowing there were innate ways to communicate without the use of an electronic or mechanical device. In the show, they would use such a device to interpret a dolphin's sounds and reply using the machine to emit similar sounds in response – in other words, speaking the dolphin's language through scientific means.

After graduating high school, I attended a secretarial program at a certificate business school in Pittsburgh, Pennsylvania. Though I enjoyed the classes – which were very professional, meaning one had to dress and act the part of working in an office – I quickly found the dorm experience wasn't for me. Those attending the business school were housed on a different campus from where our classes were held, so Monday through Friday we would trek a little over a mile down a steep road to a high-rise building along Fifth Avenue, only to walk back up that hill around five p.m. when classes ended. This made getting to know people on my campus difficult, and my roommate often stayed with friends in another building and was rarely around. I also found myself being pranked by guys who tried to scare me by calling the room and saying they knew I was alone. I would lay the phone receiver down and just wait it out, checking periodically until they finally gave up. Going home on weekends provided a much-needed respite from this lonely and uncomfortable situation.

Two months into the program, my childhood home sold sooner than anticipated and I chose to move with my parents to Georgia. However, I did get the name of a similar type of school there so I could continue with the classes I loved.

Chapter Two

THE FACES OF EXPANSION

*E*xpansion can come in many forms along our journey – be they growth-oriented, emotional, exciting, and yes, heartbreaking. These experiences come into our lives to open doors for movement, healing, and walks with deeper levels of love. Yet often we do not recognize them as such until much later in our life journeys.

At the age of nineteen, I completed a diploma program that prepared me for high-tech secretarial work, then began my first full-time job at a college in Georgia. My role involved handling incoming donations and supporting other staff members with reports from the customer relationship management or more commonly known as a CRM software system.

As I acclimated to my new life, I found that being away from my brother – who had temporarily remained in our hometown to complete his bachelor's degree – brought about challenges with communication. His jumping in to assist when

I did not know how to respond to others had become such an engrained pattern that I didn't anticipate the impact his absence would cause. Indeed, those first years in Georgia felt as though I was constantly ripping off the bandage in a big way. However, they also opened the door for me to learn how to respond to the unexpected, including open-ended questions that often left me feeling like there was a huge gap between what I knew and what I could access.

A short time later, the next cycle of trauma-like experiences began. One day, I was driving home from work; my dad, who worked at the same university, was sitting in the passenger seat. I saw that the traffic ahead of us on the two-lane road had stopped for some reason; I also became aware that the driver of the car behind us was unaware of this fact. I could feel the energy coming toward us, yet I didn't know at the time *how* I could feel it, and I was not able to voice the words to my dad. Knowing I had nowhere to go, I pushed on the brake pedal as hard as I could and waited.

I braced myself for impact as best I could by pressing the brake even harder, thinking I would at least prevent a multi-car accident. Still, the vibrations and movement from the car being pushed forward, even though it was not yet touching the car in front of me, had to go somewhere. I didn't know whether there was an impact to my body in the process, but since there were no visible injuries, neither I (nor my dad) got checked out by a doctor. It is no coincidence that I was looking in the rearview mirror, feeling that something was going to catch us unaware from behind – and, in a matter of speaking, it would a few months later. However, it wasn't until thirty-three years later that I began asking questions: Were the tremors that appeared a year or so later connected to the collision? And what message was the Universe offering through that experience?

I often learn by what I see rather than what I hear, meaning that others' actions speak much louder to me than what they say. This was in direct alignment with my early connections with the messages of dreams, animals, nature, and even some of the people around me. After my first year at the college, we began going through massive shifts in the department personnel, followed by yearly budget cuts that eliminated any open positions. This meant the remaining staff, including me, were picking up the slack. Before I knew it, I was following in my dad's footsteps (he was an administrator) by taking work home to help with the mass mailings (this was before the internet so everything was done via snail mail). I viewed it as a necessary task and chose to do it to help others in the department – without the knowledge of my boss and without pay. *This was just one example of a pattern of putting everyone else's needs ahead of my own. Other experiences would include receiving phone calls while on vacation from colleagues asking how to pull a computer report – and staying on the call for over two hours to walk them through the process. And yes, I still was an hourly employee.*

One night, a few months after the car accident and the start of the extra hours, I was awakened at three a.m. by a ringing phone. I groggily picked up and heard crying on the other end of the line. It was one of my great-aunts calling to tell

me that her sister – my paternal grandmother – had died suddenly. Through the shock, I was already thinking about how
to get ahold of my mom and dad, who were on a cruise in
the Mediterranean for their twenty-fifth wedding anniversary. I
didn't want to wake anyone at that hour, but I did decide to call
my brother, thinking he must know since he lived in the same
town as my grandparents. Imagine my surprise when I woke
him up and learned that he too was shocked! He then called
my grandfather, who didn't answer, then my great-uncle, who
said that *no one* had been able to get a hold of him.

My brother and great-uncle went over to the house, tried
knocking on the door, and then broke a window to get in,
only to be confronted by our grandfather, pistol in hand. He
also seemed a bit confused. From there, the disturbing story
unfolded. The night before, he had left the hospital after being
told by the medical staff to go home and get a good night's
sleep. My grandmother, they said, would be discharged the following day. When he got home, he took a pill to help him
sleep, which explained why he was so disoriented – and didn't
know my grandmother had passed.

My brother called me back to give me the latest, and we
agreed to be in touch when we knew something more. Our
emergency contact was my mom's sister, so I waited until six
o'clock in the morning, when I figured she'd be awake and getting my cousins breakfast. She then called the international
number to reach my parents on the ship.

Everything after that was a blur until my parents and I
arrived at the funeral home – this, after the twelve-hour drive
from Georgia to Pennsylvania. Looking back, I had likely been

in shock since receiving the phone call from my great-aunt. Now, as I walked inside, I was suddenly overcome with emotion – both mine and everyone else's that I felt in the room. Again, intuitive knowing on any level was not something that was ever talked about in our family, and probably not in our hometown. I would only become aware of my sensitivity and its connection to others decades later.

Walking into my grandparents' home after my grandmother's passing, nothing felt the same. It was too quiet, and, even with my grandfather there, void of warmth and emotion. I didn't hear her voice calling out in greeting or telling my grandfather we had arrived. The happiness was gone. On the ride to the cemetery, as I sat across from my grandfather, I was very aware of what he was feeling, how he was holding in his emotions so others wouldn't see. I also felt that hiding my own was helpful to him in that space.

My grandfather decided to move to a smaller space, so my parents and I went to help him go through and pack up the house he and my grandmother had lived in for more than seventy years. Inside those walls, an array of emotions lay dormant. Over the course of just a few days, I found myself incapable of allowing my emotions to surface as we were in a state of doing and clearing given the pressing demands of our limited time. Whatever came into their home rarely left, as there was always a perceived potential use that meant saving it for a rainy day, regardless of what the *it* was. As we separated things to trash, donate, or give to family members, we found clothing with the tags still on and often still in gift boxes, new towel sets bought and stored away, and other items kept "just in case." I'm sure this was a result of my grandparents having lived through the Great Depression, yet it left an impression on my nearly twenty-one-year-old self. It's probably why I don't like holding onto things for a rainy day. It's why if I am not wearing or using items regularly, I donate them to someone who can use them sooner rather than later.

There were many emotions trapped within those rooms. This overshadowed my own internal voices, making it a struggle to acknowledge and connect to the emotions vying for recognition to be heard or released. During the five days we spent there, I found I could not allow my body to release, through crying or on any other level. Again, too much needed to happen in the time we had available. It wasn't until we were on our way back home to Georgia, after stopping to stay overnight at a relative's house, that my body began releasing some of the pent-up energy.

About three months after the car accident, my grandmother's passing, and the holding in of my emotions, I started experiencing a tremor in my head, hands, legs, and torso. No examinations or tests were done; the doctors simply decided it was the same thing my father and grandfather had and said there was medication they could give me. I declined, only to find there were no resources for other ways to manage the emotional, mental, or physical strain of these circumstances.

It wasn't until about fifteen years later, while living in Arizona, that I finally started taking a combination of blood pressure and antiseizure medications. Though I was on it for several years, my body did not handle it well. My first experience with the antiseizure medicine was waking up in the morning and noticing that if I didn't move my body and head at the same time, I was dizzy, lightheaded, and had a sense of things within the brain shifting that felt not right – and this was at 13.5 milligrams, which I was to slowly increase to 200 milligrams a day! I felt like I was waking up in a sci-fi movie. For more than a decade, I would experiment with various foods, beverages, sweeteners, and caffeine to see what exacerbated the tremor and what had no effect. I noticed how breathing and movement played a part, as well as conscious thoughts around certain actions such as holding drinks, types of cups, and mannerisms. I recognized how the heat, dehydration, stress, and body position shifted the overall level of shaking. Any movements or motions of the hands held close to my body became increasingly irritating, limiting how often I wore makeup, jewelry, and the like.

In 1993, we suffered another loss, this time my maternal grandfather. Once again, I was the one who called my brother to share the news, as well as others who said they no longer liked getting a phone call from me because every time it was to share the passing of someone. By then, I was holding my grief emotions because I found it difficult to feel or share them with anyone, including my family, relatives, and friends.

A few years later, my mother and I had the opportunity to volunteer as photo marshals for the 1996 Olympics, handling the media photographers from all around the world at the aquatic venue. For a two-week period, Mom and I were pushed way beyond our comfort zones. I would work at my college job from 6 a.m. to 12 p.m., then we would grab the shuttle to downtown Atlanta to begin our 2 to 10 p.m. shift. We would crawl into bed around midnight, only to do the whole thing again the next day.

We had a lot of amazing experiences while part of such an international and widely watched sports event. We taped the airings daily so we could hear the commentary and see everything from a different perspective. Indeed, there was a huge difference between being on the ground and engrossed in the details of the experience and being given the big picture view, via the taped version, of the pool, activities, and overall events. I realize how important it is to view whatever situation, relationship, choice, or action from both the details and the higher view when possible. Sometimes, when we are so deep in a situation, our vision is muddied by all the perspectives and emotions, making it hard to see things clearly.

Later that same year I visited Arizona for the first time. One day, as I was window shopping in downtown historic Glendale with family and friends, I had the sudden realization that I was going to live here. I still had three years before I would be vested with the state retirement system in Georgia, and I wasn't ready to step outside the box and take a risk without that financial security and family support nearby. Yet I knew in the moment that the energy of the place felt like home.

In November of 1997, my paternal grandfather passed. Just a few days earlier he had told my dad that his three deceased brothers were visiting him and would be picking him up. After getting the news of his passing from the staff of the nursing home where he lived, my parents and I rushed over there.

Nothing had been done to change his body position or expression, and rigor was setting in – which was quite shocking and upsetting for all of us, to say the least.

Two years later, Mom and I served as co-managers of a grab-and-go hydration stand for a three-day, sixty-mile breast cancer walk. We were part of a five-woman team of volunteers who woke each morning at five to manage the fluids station, then crawled into a tent in a large field seventeen hours later. It once again pushed us both out of our comfort zones to be communication bridges between our team of women and the organizers providing status updates. Mom, who was the driver of the truck, was given a pager while I communicated via the CB radios. (The funny thing is, we are still very much like this on our trips, with my mom preferring to drive while I provide the navigation.)

The experience was much more physically demanding than we expected, taxing the body in multiple ways. We were learning that volunteer work is among the most challenging due to the unknowns. Though there were rewarding moments, and humorous things we did to make it easier on everyone else, we gave a lot of our time and energy without refilling ourselves – a lesson I wouldn't learn until close to thirty years later. When we returned home after the ceremony, I ate a quick meal then collapsed into a ten-hour sleep, only to have work the next day. My mom's massage person asked what the heck she had done as every muscle group was overly tight. Oh, the things we put our bodies through.

Chapter Three

RE-CONNECTION WITH NATURE BRINGS OPPORTUNITIES FOR EXPANSION

*S*hortly after that experience, I found a hiking trail at a nearby historic park that led through a forest-covered hillside. It had cedar bark on the ground and a switchback-type trail that went one mile straight up to a parking area and then to the last part a few hundred feet beyond. The first time I walked this trail I just couldn't go all the way. I was SO close – literally, the handrail that led to the parking lot was a few steps around a corner from where I had been the weekend before. Just that close! The day I made it the whole way to the top was my first experience of Jesus reaching out to me. I always felt most connected and accepted by Him, God, and Mother Mary while walking amongst nature.

My outer experiences were often more challenging, however. Our world wasn't quite ready for one parent who was

Catholic and the other Protestant, so finding a church where the values were merged proved impossible. Ultimately, we were taught to follow our hearts, which challenged some extended family members to come to terms with their own beliefs. I would occasionally go to mass with a friend or with my paternal grandmother and her sisters, while my brother went separately with my grandfather. For me, though, nature was my place of connection and faith. I recalled the stories of Jesus walking in the fields and connecting with those there. They were stories of acceptance, love, and understanding that had nothing to do with what you were wearing, who you were, or what you did in life. That was the faith I wanted to follow.

I had several unique adventures while out hiking and submersing myself in the environment of this trail. Beautiful large spider webs with the sun glistening off the webbing as the rays came through the trees in the early morning reminded me that beauty is found in many varying aspects of life. One day, upon descending the trail, I came to a quick halt when I saw what looked like a bear around the one tree. I went through my options: run back up the trail (knowing a bear could run faster); climb a tree, at which the bear was definitely more proficient, or just stand still and wait it out, which is what I chose. As I stood there, it started to move and with it a leash and a man appeared. The "bear" was a large chow chow dog!

This reminded me of an experience many years before while out biking with my parents in rural Pennsylvania. We had just descended a large hill when my dad turned around and started going back up. My mom and I asked what he was doing, and he said, "You'll see." We came around the corner and saw a large black bear sitting in the middle of the road. Needless to say, we too turned around! I am sure this subconscious memory had something to do with how I responded to the bear on the trail that day.

The bear symbolism would come back in when I moved to Arizona, as would other unique connections with animals – including shapeshifting, with one animal momentarily becoming another – that reopened that childhood door. I recall one time seeing a black jaguar coming toward me on a trail, then sitting down and returning to a large dog – a message that I would meet a friend who was an old soul on a trail. The dog symbolism is one of friendship and loyalty while jaguar can represent a person who is an old soul despite often their younger age.

Shortly after I moved to Arizona, I went to a local fair with my family and was drawn to a Native American tent where they were selling jewelry. I immediately became focused on wooden earrings in the shape of a bear's paw, which went home with me. The bear often showed up in my dreams to remind me to walk in its footsteps, go within, or find time to hibernate which can be seen as a form of meditation.

I had other experiences with domestic animals many years before I began my business. Back in Georgia, I remember deeply connecting with my sister-in-law's cat, who would sleep with me every time I stayed at their apartment. Though I couldn't describe it I do recall thinking there was something special about our relationship. Clarity would come later, through other felines and canines who had their own teachings to deliver.

As I worked toward getting vested, I was also taking steps to set myself up for future success – though I didn't share my thoughts with any family, friends, or colleagues. I bought and paid off a new vehicle, and when my parents expressed a desire that I move into the home they had built for retirement, I instead decided to purchase my first home, a condo, on my own.

In July of 1999, I handed a letter of resignation to my boss that included two proposals: I could leave in two weeks, or I could stay until December 1. At the time we were in constant hiring freezes, so when a position was vacated it had to remain empty for three months before it could even be advertised, let alone filled – and I was the only one who knew the customer relationship management software inside and out. It was important to me to not leave people in the lurch, despite some of the challenging times we had throughout the years. No surprise, my boss took me up on my offer to stay and I began creating a step-by-step manual for the software down to every tab, space, and click of the enter key, with visual aids for additional assistance. This manual would still be in use five years later by a whole new crew of people.

I also spent several months training the existing staff, including the department head and directors, on how to use the system. I would then tell the five remaining people the reason they were learning the system. It was an emotional time, as I was not only leaving this family, but my blood relatives and friends to challenge myself in a whole new way. I know my mom, dad, and I struggled with being separated from each other after spending these past twelve years in Georgia as a trio facing the new together.

Chapter Four

A LEAP OF FAITH

*A*t age thirty, I moved to Arizona to start a new adventure thousands of miles away from everyone and everything I had ever known. My only acquaintances in Arizona were a couple who were family friends that initially had lived near mine in Pennsylvania and moved out West years earlier.

It was a challenging three-and-a-half months of reviewing job ads, sending cover letters and applications – and doing my best to not feel like I needed to be home 24/7 waiting for the phone to ring (this was before the days when everyone had a cell phone and email was just taking hold). Fortunately, I had saved up enough to live for several months, and in fact it would be four months before I connected to a job ad that just felt right. I hand-delivered the cover letter and resume to the college human resources office and received word that an interview was being scheduled. I was offered the position a few days later and began the job on April 10, 2000.

The couple I knew had adopted a Great Dane-bloodhound pup from a local animal shelter. He'd had a rough beginning, in and out of shelters, with one set of adoptees calling him "Diablo," which did not match his gentle, loving, and sweet personality. He came into my friends' home with his own suitcase of early trauma, including being fearful of men and hats. His new human dad and brothers were sad that he was afraid of them, as all they wanted was to love him. All the pup wanted was to be loved for who he was, but he didn't recognize their efforts because he had never experienced it before.

We became fast friends. We were both unknowingly searching for acceptance, love, and friendship – and that is what we discovered in each other. I visited with his family and then we would play out in the yard, with me continuously throwing a ball or rubbing his paw that he would place upon my arm as we sat near one another.

When he didn't want to eat his dinner, they called me to come over and help. I would sit on the floor and pick up some morsels of food, watching them disappear as I talked to him friend to friend. Sometimes we just need someone who understands us on a soul level, not needing to know why but just wanting to feel the love and connection from someone who gets us.

He always knew how I was feeling, despite my constant pronouncement that, "Everything is just fine" (I even connected this phrase to the letter's "EJF" on my license plate as a way to remember it. While writing this I recognized the need to change the meaning of this acronym as it is no longer suited to who I am becoming.) The pup felt beneath the surface of my words and into the hidden compartments of my heart, sensing my deep-seated emotions that other people did not.

Sometimes his four-legged cousins – a male and a female rottweiler – would join us. I always felt and saw the gentle nature of the male, who many relatives and friends were afraid to be around. I also sensed the questioning, from him and his sister, about the whys. I did the best I could at the time to help them understand that sometimes people are more willing to believe the stories of others than their own experiences. This made me realize that all of us – two-legged, four-legged, feathered, and finned – are on journeys to discover acceptance of who we are. Some would continue to allow their truths or beliefs to be clouded by those stories, whether we hear them from people we know or perfect strangers.

The pup and I had many fun experiences together through play, connection, and toys. When I arrived at his house and rang the doorbell, I would hear his parents inside the house asking him who was at the door, and I could feel his excitement growing while the smile on my face also grew bigger. Upon seeing me he would race to his toy bin, digging around for the one toy I'd gotten him for a holiday gift, then he'd dart back to greet me, ready for play. Before long, he and his parents moved away, and I would see him only one more time, several years later just before he crossed the Rainbow Bridge. He was much older and nearly blind, yet he remembered my gentle touch.

We often wonder about the reason others come into our lives. What I have learned throughout my years of working directly with the animal beings is that it does not matter whether we are talking about humans or other species – they are there for a reason, a season, or a lifetime. The pup and I came together when we needed friendship and acceptance for who we were – and it was not ever about species.

A little while later, a few other animal kids would arrive in my life through trips to visit my brother and his family. After hugging the people in the family, I always walked around to connect with the animal companions. The canines often beat their human family members to the hugs, while many of the felines would wait for me in the other rooms to connect and receive love. One kid in the form of an all-black cat slept behind a bathroom door. I would gently open the door, calling him and listening to his responding purr as I connected with him before moving on to visit with the family.

During my time there, I slept on the family room couch and often woke up to find my "behind the door" buddy staring softly yet intently at me. This is when I began to learn about the power of energy, though I did not recognize it as such until much later, after learning Reiki. He and I had these special midnight chat sessions when he would accept my love and touch, which was unusual any other time. After ten or fifteen minutes, I would turn off the light and tell him goodnight before drifting gently back to sleep with ease. A very special, and very unique, friendship!

His brother, who was much more senior, taught me different lessons about perceptions and boundaries. He truly was a character! His main lesson in his later years was that just because he chose to claim your lap did not mean he was open for touch. Usually, if one of us had the audacity to think in that manner, he would lash out or hiss. If you're wondering why we would want said kitty to grace us with his presence, it was because occasionally he'd surprise us by permitting such a gesture of love and affection.

Chapter Five

WALKING WITH CHANGE
FROM WITHIN

At the college in Arizona, I served as a liaison – or "bridge," as I called it – between my department and several others, including information technology, marketing, finance, accounting, and the registrar. With time, I would take on the tasks that others did not want – ones that helped the department move quicker from marketing to sales by editing the backend of website page code with new dates, content, and the like, which also assisted the marketing department as they did not need to allocate a person to keep up with my department's requests. Then it was working with collecting data from various directors in-house and in our international locations for several annual rankings processes.

Four years later, the next cycle of relatives passing began, with an uncle with whom I had a very close relationship. We were on the same wavelength and had similar styles. He would sit in a rocking chair in the room where everyone else was hanging out, seemingly buried in a book but aware of the conversation and jumping in when he chose to.

When I first heard of his passing I wasn't sure I could make it to his funeral, which was across the country. However, the next day I knew I was meant to be there and that I was to take a teddy bear from his childhood that he had gifted to me when I was little. Into the suitcase it went, though I didn't share with anyone that I was bringing it. I then called my mom to let her know I would be flying in the next day. When I showed up at my maternal grandmother's house, where my uncle had lived after the passing of my grandfather, the first thing my grandmother asked was if I had brought my uncle's teddy bear! Yes, the subconscious message had gotten through to me. Most likely it wouldn't have come through had I flown with my mom the day before.

Two years later, a second uncle would leave us, followed by a third five years later – all in late February and early March, which made this time of year exceedingly difficult. It was so very hard for my grandmother to lose three of her ten children before her. I felt and sensed the bottled-up pain while she spoke of not knowing how to cry anymore. I can relate to that in the power of loss. Be it people, animal friends, jobs, or changes in the ways of life – loss is felt through a cycle or staging of emotions, often in no particular order. Sometimes it is seen and felt by others witnessing our grief and other times it is processed solely within us – but that doesn't mean it is any less deep.

As I began feeling the energy more and tuning into the signs that were all around me, it became increasingly difficult to stay in the status quo. Following my intuition would reach a new level when a new department head took over and had much of the staff interviewing for their current positions – with the possibility of not getting them. We could interview for other positions if we desired, with the understanding that if we got it we were potentially putting a colleague out of a job. Talk about stress! At the same time, we were being given a parallel message about reframing, finding work-life balance, and finding time to breathe and exercise. It felt like there were two very different paths with no point of intersection between them.

During this time, I felt drawn to a very unique yet unspoken calling – one that was not on paper or directed by the department head and his team. It was from a much higher source, one that guided me to hear my innermost voice, which led me not to interview but to support and touch base with everyone who was feeling the pressure. There was so much anxiety; I felt it, so very present and intense, the moment I opened the door to walk into our building each morning. Going with the flow and feeling peace, which was my inner compass, directed me to take a personal risk – and step outside my comfort zone – to connect, communicate, and be a supportive sounding board for various people in this space. The two people I was most drawn to support from the start of this process were the two that at the conclusion of the interviews lost their positions.

At this time, I did not view my actions from the perspective of the higher-ups in our department. Now, reflecting upon this experience, I can see that they may have potentially questioned my perceived non-action as indicating I was not the type-A personality that was always striving for more

– but "more" is in the eye of the beholder. At this point, I was searching for more balance in my outer world, which I later recognized as a calling for deep inner harmony. This higher call to action from Spirit gave me a voice to be of service to others in a time of challenge while I received that feeling of peace and harmony my heart craved.

This began a new cycle of getting lots of messages and signs from Spirit in a variety of manners. My life outside work was also changing, as were the lives of my family members. The most significant of those changes occurred in 2012, when my parents, who had retired to Arizona, opened their home to my maternal grandmother when it was determined that, due to declining health, she could no longer live alone.

Within a short period of time, my dad and grandmother began experiencing similar things. Both had back pain show up at the same time. Now, I understand the body and its messages more clearly, and I know the back often has to do with a person's foundation; therefore, back pain can result from challenges surrounding living in a new place or finding yourself, your time, and your schedule are no longer yours. Living together had pushed my family to reidentify themselves and what they knew to be true. This was especially so for my grandmother, who found herself where she never wanted to be – living with one of her kids. Yes, one or another of her children had moved in with her at various times after my grandfather's passing, but for some reason, she hadn't seen it as the same.

This time was also incredibly challenging for my mom, who felt torn between my dad and my grandmother and their individual needs. Things would come to a head in early 2012, when both ended up going into the hospital within days of each other for back issues. In fact, on the day my grandmother was discharged, my dad ended up in the very same room! My mom called me for help and asked which one I wanted to be with as both needed constant assistance. I picked my grandmother, in part because I knew I could provide the help she required, but also because we had a really close relationship – the result of our rooming together on several family trips after my grandfather's passing.

Chapter Six

BIG CHANGES ON THE HORIZON

*T*he next phase of my journey had a mixture of highs and lows, a series of fun and exciting times along with moments of busting through walls and pushing past insecurities. Life was about to change in monumental ways and through a variety of circumstances.

In late 2012, I completed a series of tandem skydives – a bold step in addressing the anxiety, and a fear of heights, that had resulted from that childhood fall. I wanted to overcome these challenges and the vertigo-type feelings I experienced in my body when looking down, or even watching a program that took the camera over the edge of a building or other high vantage point. Doing these jumps mirrored the fall, opening a door for me to begin trusting others as well as myself, which helped me get through the next phase of walking hand in hand with change from within.

Eighteen months later I sensed big changes on the horizon, triggering me to sell my house, move into a smaller rental with a lower payment and fewer expenses overall. Four short months after a restructuring at the college, I received an email from the department head's administrative assistant scheduling an appointment but with no information about what the meeting was about – which was odd and red flag number one. When I went to my immediate supervisor asking if she knew anything about the appointment it was obvious that I'd caught her off guard. The feeling that she knew and couldn't tell me was the second red flag, and I knew before I even entered the department head's office that my position was being eliminated. On June 30, 2013, I would find myself standing in the parking lot, not knowing what tomorrow would bring. I had just entered a space of possibilities as vast and overwhelming as the shampoo aisle of the grocery store.

On the afternoon of Tuesday, July 16, less than two weeks after this job loss, I had a very important visit with my maternal grandmother. This visit, during which three generations of female family members came together, was the first time since my grandmother moved out to Arizona that I saw her truly happy and joy-filled. She was giddy and talking like a childhood friend – a side of her I had not seen much of since my grandfather transitioned twenty years prior.

The next day my mother called with a curious piece of information: my grandmother had begun kissing family photos, mainly of those who had passed. Three days after that, while standing in my kitchen, I got a visual of my grandmother seated amongst those who had departed. "Oh," I said aloud, "it's like you are having a family reunion!" I looked at the clock and a few minutes later I got a call from my mom sharing that my grandmother had transitioned at the time the image appeared.

Through my dreams, I began receiving messages about my grandmother's location while she waited for the family to gather for the funeral service in Florida. She shared with me what the building and place looked like, how her body felt there, and other details. She even joked that for, the first time, she arrived first!

After my parents and I flew there, I saw the place for the first time, and was able to confirm what she'd shared with me during the nocturnal visitations. I found myself for the third time after a relative's death riding with one of my uncles as he drove directly behind the hearse on the way to the cemetery. It was a very surreal experience, but I sensed there was a higher perspective aspect to it that, at the time, seemed just out of my grasp. Later, I would discover that I was seen as a guide or one who walked with others through major life changes, taking them to the bridge of whatever their next experience was.

A week or so after returning from the funeral, I sent a letter to my previous boss, expressing gratitude to him for ending my employment. I told him that we never truly understand how one decision will impact another's life, and his decision had made it possible for me to visit with my grandmother that day, when she was the happiest she had been in a long time. Also, while his decision had closed one door, it had opened another door to a future role not yet fully defined or understood by me. Writing the letter felt good, though the truth of the matter was that I did not know where my next steps would take me. I was entering the darkness and beginning a journey to learn who I would become.

Initially, I worked with a career office that helped me walk through the unexpected grief associated with this loss. The triggers of pain, anger, and emptiness came from seemingly unlikely places: a banner in an airport terminal, being in my car, and just working through the career process to identify my skills. Then came the moment I just knew I was not meant to continue with the same type of career. I could no longer do something just to have a j-o-b; I had to do something I loved, and I had to discover what that was. I knew I was meant to learn things in a different type of educational setting, the one called life.

That was the first large leap in this new experience and would place me on my new journey of venturing into the unknowns of self-employment. I will be honest – there have been times when I thought about looking for another position at a college, just to be safe. I will also say I have learned so much about myself, my drive, determination, and challenges on the emotional roller coaster of self-employment and one that continues with each breath I take. This is what my path to healing looks like as, yet another piece is placed in the puzzle. So much of this experience is tied to mindset, which I have found can be monumental and detrimental in the same breath, depending on whether we are in alignment with our personal truth or not.

Chapter Seven

A GENERATION ENDS

$\mathcal{M}$y grandmother's crossing opened an internal water valve, with tears releasing every time I got in my car to travel to or from some place. Somehow, the forward motion of the car seemed to open a channel for these emotions to flow. The car signified a new step in my life and my grieving as it put me "out in the public" – seen and yet not seen. It was like all the pent-up emotions of losing seven relatives – plus seven colleagues who had passed during that timeframe – rose to the surface, pushing for release from me, from my grandmother, and from anyone else from whom I had taken on emotions without knowing how to process the experiences. For during those shifts in relationships, deaths, and positions held brought about so much to process and release from the grief held within the organs, mind, and emotions of the body.

Even now, as I write this book, I feel a twinge appear at the back of my right lung area, which energetically or emotionally is connected to grief. Any experience of loss – be it a loved one, friend, pet, or a job, or moving to a new place away from family and friends – can result in grief responses. The thoughts that arose during my "car therapy" sessions often included questions as to why I was still here, for on a certain level I felt left behind by those who had transitioned. Some thoughts were upsetting, even dark, and led me into periods of depression and emptiness. More than ever before, I understood the line from the movie *E.T.*, when Eliott spoke about the pain of separation and not knowing how to feel after this type of loss. For me, this separation marked the true ending of a cycle. Not only was I grieving the people and my job, but my sense of certainty as to where I was heading. So much of our lives and experiences are tied to other people, situations, and places, and when we lose them it is like our "muscle memory" link to our environment, and even to ourselves, is lost.

Chapter Eight

VENTURING INTO THE UNKNOWN

 y journey to self-employment started with working out of a spiritual center and spiritual fairs, initially offering Reiki sessions. Later, I expanded my offerings to
include hand reflexology treatments and meditation classes at
the center, which helped me move from the behind-the-scenes
roles I'd held my first forty-four years of life to begin the process of being heard and seen. It was scary – yet so worthwhile!
– and something I needed to do for my own soul's journey
because I had never been one to put myself in the public eye. I
recall in high school not liking to sell stuff door to door, even
to relatives and neighbors I knew, for it felt like stepping into
the unknown in a huge way.

During each experience at the fairs and the center, I was learning more about being seen and acquiring the confidence to be
uncomfortable in my own skin as I re-educated myself on who I
was and where I was going. It was challenging and in many ways

took me back to recreating the foundation I had built over the thirteen years at the business school in Arizona and the twelve previous years at a college in Georgia. I was certainly pushed out of my comfort zone that first year, 2014, when I made a total of $500! This would increase slowly as I learned about me, the world I was entering, and, later, the necessary switch in mindset to place value, not only on the services but the value of my time and what I innately brought to the role.

There were also fears that held me stuck in an invisible cage of my own making. Understanding that I held the key would take many years of processing, releasing, and opening the new doors that presented themselves on my path. There were messages from people I worked with at these fairs that held real meaning and have stayed with me throughout the years. One example was the man who told me that I couldn't save and cure everyone – a hard lesson for me as it was instinctual to want to do so. I now keep the focus on what is in the highest and greatest good of the receiver and the knowledge that the result may not be what I want for the other. In essence, you can do everything in your power, but if it is one's time there is nothing that will hold them here.

I learned the Usui Reiki beginning in 2009 through 2011 and other energy modalities such as Blue Star Celestial Reiki, along with a few others, later. In 2014, I took an additional series of classes, including Animal Reiki and Animal Communication held in an environment of wild animal beings, that brought me closer to the animal and natural worlds. Following these teachings, I began visiting local wild animal parks with the objective of seeing who wanted to connect and receive the healing energy on some level. This quickly became a favorite activity and one filled with so much love and respect for their contributions to the world – and my opportunity to give back and nurture the animal kingdom in a way that went far beyond walking through a park.

One of my first experiences led me to a herd of Oryx that I asked, via my heart, if they were interested in receiving some energy healing. The gatekeepers of the group parted ways to allow a more senior member to come forth and stand just on the other side of the fencing that surrounded their enclosure. I sat about fifteen feet away and focused the energy with the intention for his highest good and for love to surround him. He stayed there, choosing to receive for twenty minutes until one of the three gatekeepers came forward to move him along. It was such a beautiful and heart-warming encounter with these wild ones.

The next involved a group of fish and turtles in an open tank of water just inside the door of a building on the property. As I entered, I heard and felt the vibrations as children ran up and down the hallway laughing, yelling, and playing. It sounded so loud – almost deafening. I turned to the tank, knelt down a bit, and inquired if they were interested in receiving Reiki, to which I got a resounding yes as all but one came to my side of the tank. They stayed focused on me for ten minutes. When we are present and open to infinite possibilities, we can experience amazing connections and gifts with those in the natural world.

There were many people, including family members, that I felt tested by during this time. They did not understand this new career exploration that for me felt like I was discovering a new land, new culture, and new beings with a new language. Oftentimes they would ask others for insights on my choices before coming back around to me. I learned with time that my part in their understanding was sharing the seeds and not feeling responsible for their reaction or response, just as a classroom teacher can provide information with no guarantee that all students will actually receive it in the same exact way or will understand it in the moment it is provided. I will say it was a very challenging several years as I worked through accepting others' reactions and judgments, especially since I had always supported their ideas and forward progress.

After self-publishing my first book, *Are You Picking Up Your Messages,* I realized that writing was the only way I knew how to share what I was embarking on with family, friends, and colleagues. Still, sharing it through the spoken word was a deep-seated challenge for me – maybe I was just learning to accept me and where I was in this new journey. Doing this type of self-work, as well as traversing this unfamiliar terrain, gave me the longitude to be available for the next unexpected step on my path.

Chapter Eight

THE HEART OPENS

*W*hen every step you take is outside your norm, things don't surprise you as much.

In the latter part of 2014, my dad had a heart attack while being out on a long walk with Mom around their neighborhood. He just said he didn't feel like he could take another step, his legs were feeling SO heavy, and could not catch his breath. They lived in a retirement community in which people lived independently but could get more care when needed. They called the onsite EMT, who called 911 and my dad was transported within ten minutes of the attack.

When I got to the hospital, he was having a heart catheterization; they also put in a second stent in the same location as his first: the left anterior descending artery. Following this, he began a six-week rehab, going to the hospital three days a week, to learn how to cope with the apprehension and anxiety that would surface in the days and weeks afterward. As it turned out, the next year would be hell for my dad and those walking the journey with him. His ejection fraction, which is one of the methods for telling how the heart is doing, was at 15 to 20 percent. This number was scary, partly because we didn't know what it meant, but, more importantly, as it was unknown from before the heart attack. The perception is that we come in with a perfect 100, which is false. There was so much fear around this situation that it showed up in every experience.

My dad's cardiologist suggested that he wear a defibrillator vest all the time – the only exception being when he was in the shower. This caused additional fear and panic on so many levels. Let me explain. These vests detect certain changes in the heart and sound an alert, meaning the wearer must respond quickly to either turn it off or allow it to deliver the shock. Now, on the surface that sounds good, but for someone like my dad – who was afraid of the device, afraid he wouldn't need it if it alerted him, and afraid he would not press the buttons correctly due to heightened nerves and the essential tremor exacerbated by nervousness – it is a nightmare. Now, not only was he fearful of having another heart attack, he was fearful of the vest that could save his life.

I understood his fears, as I also had been diagnosed with an essential tremor and could see my dad's predicament through my own eyes. To me, it was a no-win situation, like a ticking time bomb that could go off at any time. In the end, Dad decided he couldn't use it. His doctor was furious with him, saying he was sealing his fate, and the vest was the only way to stop another heart attack from occurring.

Shortly after this experience, my dad changed his cardiologist, which was the best thing he could do for himself. His new doctor was able to understand why the vest had been prescribed, yet also had the compassion to understand my dad's fears and the added obstacle of the tremor. He didn't sugarcoat the fact that, in addition to an enlarged heart, my dad had experienced a *catastrophic heart attack*. This term would be used regularly in the years after, and we individually worked on managing how we responded to these early triggering descriptions.

In addition to dealing with Dad's health, I continued during this year to learn to be okay with who and where I was in this new life. Other members of the spiritual community would "randomly" stop and tell me I belonged there, or that I was in the right place. At the time, I wondered what my "tell" was, yet it was good to hear and it offered support when I needed it most.

The next year was a constant walk of not ever knowing what was around the next corner. Dad was obviously still anxious and fearful of having another heart attack, but his focus was now on figuring out how and when to take all his new prescription medications and working through the early panic attacks that would send us to the emergency room.

In January of 2015, my dad went into the hospital to have a pacemaker / defibrillator placed in his body, which seemed to provide him some peace of mind, along with weekly visits to see his primary care physician and his cardiologist.

Around the same time, I had the chance opportunity to assist a friend who had been called out of town and needed someone to watch her pets. Little did I know that this would open a whole new possibility for me. It brought me so much joy when her reserved cat began coming into the room where I sat to connect with me. This was my first entrance into doing pet visits, which would continue later with overnights with the canine friend.

At the local spiritual fairs, I found that working with hand reflexology provided a closeness and connecting point to open up to the intuitive communication that was beginning to flow in. That said, it was still challenging to tap into the port that allowed me to fully hear and vocalize my intuitive awareness to reach and share from that place. I was apprehensive about not conveying something correctly, which further blocked the information. Oftentimes, I felt as if I hadn't been given the access code.

Between March and August, we were at four different hospitals in the metro area for various situations with my dad. I would get the calls in the middle of the night and ask where I was heading before grabbing clothes and rolling out the door. In an opportunity to find balance amongst the ever-shifting landscape of the healthcare world, my mother and I went on a spiritual retreat together to find healing and nurturing for ourselves. It allowed us to learn something new, do something supportive, and care for our bodies, minds, and spirits in a space that didn't put us through some level of shock.

After the retreat, we had planned a weekend get-together with two aunts who were flying in for Mom's birthday, only to have to cancel when Dad landed back in the hospital for a hernia operation. Mom and I spent all day, every day with him. The night before his surgery I asked him if he'd like some Reiki to help with the anxiety he was experiencing. After his consent I did the session while my mom prayed for him. That evening we left the hospital and headed in our separate cars to a coffee shop to decompress and process everything. When she got to the coffee shop, Mom shared that she had prayed, specifically asking for my paternal grandmother's help in keeping my dad relaxed throughout the night. She then noticed the vanity license plate on the car ahead of her – it read "Nana is Here"! Now, Nana is what my brother and I called my dad's mother. Yes, our loved ones in spirit are always there for us; we need only ask.

On the day of Dad's surgery, he told me that he wished he knew that his parents were with him. We talked about it for a while, then the surgical prep nurse came into the room, looked at Dad's hospital wristband, and told him that her grandmother's name was Vizzini too. She then went on to say that her grandmother came from Sicily and my dad said his father had too. After she left the room, I told him that he had the answer to his question. His mother had shown herself via a license plate to Mom immediately after she'd asked for her assistance; now, he had gotten another confirmation from the nurse, with the name and the Sicily connection. I believe he found peace in that knowledge.

As we entered August my dad got a nosebleed that wouldn't stop – a side effect of the blood thinners he was taking – and landed back in the emergency room. They shoved packing in his nose and then transported him to a hospital in downtown Phoenix, twenty-five miles away, as that was the only hospital in the area with an ENT specialist on staff. He would spend several more days there, and Mom and I decided that when we knew how to get to the cafeteria we had been there too long. The hospitals in general, with all the computer monitors, lights, noises, emotions, and general energy, were very draining. We were not yet at the point of recognizing that we needed to refill our joy for ourselves, but we did work to find some aspect of humor to lighten the weight of these environments. Humor was my dad's normal, so it seemed appropriate to lean in that direction to lift our energy and break through the heaviness.

PART II

Love Finds A Door

Chapter Nine

AN INTUITIVE IDEA SPARKS ACTION

*I*n November of 2015, while taking an intuitive development class, a monumental realization and message came
through to help form a new idea and path forward for me.
Whenever I was out and about, I would get such joy when I
saw an animal in any form. I was always seeing movement, out
of the corner of my eye, by a bird, dog, cat, hummingbird, or
any other animal – no matter where I was or what people I
was with. I decided to take that enjoyment a step further and
began researching what I needed to do to turn it into something tangible.

By April of 2016, I had licensed my business, Dream Pet
Care, LLC, with the state, got it insured and bonded, chose the
accounting software and the pet-sitting software that would
be used to house the client information, and took a certificate
program through an international pet-sitting company to learn
more about the care of animals and how to set up the business

side of it. I had also taken a pet first aid class. After working at multiple colleges where the appropriate computer software was only thought of after creating multiple manual systems, I knew it needed to be identified before the people arrived.

The naming of the business was the most challenging, as every time I came up with one, an online search or check for licensing revealed that it was already being used in some fashion. At the time, I did not want to use my personal name as I was not ready to be seen on that level. I finally asked for assistance from my angels and crossed-over loved ones and heard, every day for a week, the song "Somewhere Over the Rainbow," which I always connected with my paternal grandmother in spirit. It was playing in my head when I woke up, over the radio at a restaurant, when I opened a social media platform, and at a coffee shop, where a band played it live! The business name "Over the Rainbow" was taken, but my attention was drawn to the line about "daring to dream." And – just like that – *Dream Pet Care* was born.

The start of my pet sitting/pet companion business would emerge with my intuition clicking certain pieces of the current life puzzle and struggles into place. What I did not yet understand was that this would be a journey of love, communication, and healing. It would take me through personal and professional challenges, family health obstacles, and a deep dive into my relationship with myself, as well as the animal beings with whom I would connect through my visits. I had always loved animals, but the real learning over these first seven years in business has been about the true meaning and depth of unconditional love – with the animal and nature beings, other people, and the rarest of all, oneself.

In the early days of this process, I volunteered at a local animal shelter, mainly hanging out with the felines as it seemed that's who needed my services at the time. There were fewer volunteers who visited with this group as it was perceived that they required less interaction and support. In addition, my ears were way too sensitive to be in a closed-off group room with the dogs for too long due to the loud barking. Indeed, I quickly found that the felines were a better fit for my body in this environment. More important was the realization that an aspect of me other people seemed to look down upon was readily accepted in the animal kingdom.

One day, when the felines and I were hanging out, I silently said, *Maybe I am too quiet.* Immediately, they showed me through their actions what I had already intuitively picked up from them: that my silence was a gift, and a very useful one in specific circumstances.

At some point, a gentleman and his young son came in to see the cats, and I explained to him that there were others in the outside cattery. We sat down out there, and I fell into my normal quiet space, observing the felines who were assisting me that day to understand my silence as a *gift*. A few moments later, the man began speaking about how he'd returned from an overseas military mission several months earlier. He spoke about how challenging it was to return, get back into society, and work through some health situations. Coming to the shelter was about the love and support he found with the animal beings. They offered a calming space for him to work through whatever surfaced in the moment.

It was then that I understood the cats' message. People find a sounding board in beings – be they human, animal, or nature – that appear quiet; they provide a willing ear that opens the door for people to be and feel at ease – and allow the flow of their words a safe place to land without fear of judgment. Being a quiet being is a gift because it allows others to be received and accepted for who and where they are in that moment. People can bare their souls to an animal companion as there is no fear of it going elsewhere. Your pets and animal friends hear you, support you, and love you – *unconditionally*.

Over the year-and-a-half that I spent time at the shelter, those animal beings taught me many great lessons around accepting myself – though I didn't always recognize them as such until much later. I also found ways to support them individually in their experience of waking up and finding themselves at an unknown place without their people, who had either passed away or left them at the shelter because they were not able to take the cat or dog with them to their next destination. In the latter situation, I wondered if those people, had they been able to feel the pain that I did from these beings, would have found a way to do so, though I also know we do the best we can with the options available.

An emotional memory surfaced in the editing of this book about a situation that occurred when I was nine or ten. We had two cats and this situation necessitated that we leave them for a time on my uncle's farm. We did not know whether they would be there when we returned. This was before the time of pet sitters and resorts, and neighbors were rarely asked. Indeed, we only saw the cats once more, and briefly, so again, I understand our choices are not always what we'd hope.

There were so many from whom I felt the pain, the emptiness, grief, and heartache around the loss of their people, as well as fear of the unknown yet to come. It was so hard to see them hurting in that manner and I felt their pain on every level of my being. I was also learning that I had to be very grounded and aware of my energy when working with those who needed this level of love, compassion, and friendship. There were days when I would leave after three or four hours, completely drained because I'd unknowingly given all my energetic reserves to them just as I often did with people – this is where I first began offering animal Reiki to those pets who wanted to receive it.

One day, I was sitting in a chair across from a kennel where a new arrival sat in his bed, his back to the room. In my lap sat a female cat, who recognized what I was offering and took in what she needed before jumping down to climb inside the kennel. She let him know it was okay to receive and helped move it to him. She came back over to move the energy once again to the newbie before he began to relax to a certain degree. In the days ahead, he was more open to contact from the other animal beings (though not yet people at this stage) – as evidenced by a noticeable change in his stature. A few days later, he was more open to being out and about with the other cats.

Some days, just before closing, I would ask if they wished to receive the Reiki. About ten would sit down on the floor near me while I sent the energy to them, both hands-on and via distance. When they were done getting as much as each chose, they individually came over to acknowledge the gift of love and healing, with some licking my hands or rubbing up against me and purring in gratitude. Often the ways we can assist them on their paths come in the form of something they recognize.

Chapter Ten

SCHOOL'S IN SESSION

The first pet visit assignments began even before my business was fully licensed. Someone I met through the intuitive development class had not taken a family vacation for years as they didn't want to leave their two dogs home alone at night. When they learned I would be offering overnights, they decided to give it a try. Many of my clients were first-timers, so we were learning together.

My first meeting with the two dogs was a unique and amazing experience. When I arrived they were being kept in the kitchen by gates because they were SO *excited* to meet people that they were *talking* and doing their best to be heard over their mom as she opened the door to let me in. After a greeting with these vivacious kids, they settled down some while she filled me in on their daily routine. She also told me about a feline living in the home, adding that I would rarely see him. He tended to stay in one of two spaces rather than interacting with the family members – especially since the dogs were added to the household mix.

I asked the mom to show me where he generally hung out so I could meet him. We went back to where he was napping, and he opened his eyes to look at me. I introduced myself to him before letting him sniff me and I allowed him to choose the level of engagement, not touching him at that point.

I told him, "I will be visiting with you and your sisters in a couple of days. If you want to hang out in your rooms that is okay, but you are welcome to join us if you like."

His mom and I then went back to the kitchen to continue the meet-and-greet. Five minutes later the feline came in and over to me, rubbing up against my leg. His mom was surprised and said just how unusual this was, especially since he remained with us for the rest of my visit. Before leaving their home, I told the animal kids when I would return, and it was only then that the feline wandered back to his sleeping space.

When I showed up for my initial visit, I heard the girls, the pups, yelling at me as I walked in. They were happy to see a buddy – as was the feline, who joined us in the kitchen. We spent that first visit learning a bit about each other, with that connection deepening each time I returned. The feline again came out to greet me when I returned to give the housekey back to their mom, then he walked back to his room of choice when I left. This became his routine during later assignments with the crew; in fact, he would take this to the next level by walking me to the door!

What I discovered was just how much my cat friend loved the frequency-style music I played while I was there with them. He would sit adjacent to it for as long as I played it. Often the four of us would connect through a meditative space with the tones, which allowed me to shift into their normal state of presence and opened a door for deeper connection and understanding in their form of communication.

There were a variety of teachings this gang shared with me, though one in particular came in a very unique way. At the time I was working through self-imposed lessons – and though I did not understand their origin I did know I was being guided to break through. One fall weekend on a full moon night, a personal wall would come into the physical world with the help of a faulty door lock. There are many situations we pet care professionals hope not to find ourselves in – and this was one of them; however, no matter how diligent we are, we cannot always anticipate every situation.

Over the course of this weekend, I was in and out of this slider door at least ten times a day without an issue… until that night when the lock slipped, causing us (or, to be precise, me) to get locked out of the house. One of the pups was tall, so I tried to get her to push up on the lever after she re-entered the house through their doggy door. When this was unsuccessful, I brainstormed options, which were extremely limited as my cell phone was inside (and playing music to entertain the cat), as were my keys and those for the house. I always re-lock doors after I enter the homes as a natural instinct, and never in the brainstorming process did I think of breaking a window.

I soon found myself eyeing the doggy door, then looking at the height and width of the larger dog's body and comparing it to my hips and shoulders. I sent out an inquiry to my spiritual team as to whether this would work and got a yes, so it would seem on this night I was meant to physically go through a wall! Luckily, this one was behind a block wall fence surrounding the yard near a streetlight and not in a glass door! The larger of the two dogs always had the personality of a cheerleader, and that night was no different. For the first time in my career I heard a dog bark seemingly from a distance behind me while immediately receiving the English translation. Any time I would hesitate or question the action, I would hear her say, "You got this…keep going!" My feline friend waited and watched over me from inside the house, and when I finally wiggled my way in and landed on the kitchen floor, all three ran over to nuzzle my hair while saying, "You did it!"

A celebratory dance, animal style, followed, with a lot of happy faces and jumping. After this I kept the slider partially open any time we went into the yard. The first time one of the dogs asked why I was doing that when I now knew I could get in. My reply: "Just because there is a known way in doesn't mean I want to have to do it again – plus I have bruises up and down my legs to show for it!"

Lessons come in a variety of experiences. This one was on multiple levels, both personally and professionally. Now I memorize door codes and make sure to have pants with pockets so I can keep the key on me.

Two years later, I would have a new language experience with these animal kids when I entered their house and found a "gift" in the form of a dead, underground mammal. By then I'd had many visits with them and they had never done this before so I wondered what was up. Upon contacting their parents, I learned this had been going on for about two months. Had something, I asked, changed in the household at that time? Had there been any discussions that the kids may have interpreted in a different way? Turns out they had heard something about one of them moving out and some other stuff that made them think they needed to show their love in another way. Of course, their parents didn't know this and started to close the doggy door at night in an attempt to eliminate the behavior.

Once I understood what was triggering them, I sat them down and said aloud, "Your love is enough; you do not need to bring me gifts. I will let your parents know what is going on, but I cannot make any promises. If you agree to leave the other gifts outside, I will leave the doggy door open at night."

I did not have another incident the whole time I was there!

Animals hear everything – and they interpret it the best they can, considering that whatever human language they're listening to is not their native tongue. One thing we can do is keep the line of communication open (to the best of our ability) to help them understand "why" something is happening. We can do this by looking softly into their eyes while speaking to them with simple words, as you might with a younger child. This way they will better understand what is occurring and why. Repetition may be necessary as they work to understand our words and reasoning.

Later, during a house remodeling project, I learned about one of the dogs' ultrasensitive ears. The cat also did not like the noises or the vibrations from the various equipment; the pup barked the whole time at the unknown noise. The more I was around the dog during this process, the more I tuned into her and what she was feeling and when. When I realized that I was "feeling" the sound of the nail gun in my chest, I looked her in the eyes and said aloud, "Here's where I feel it. Is that where you feel it?" She looked at me and acknowledged my question with a blink of her eyes. Blinking is often a way for pets to answer yes. I shared with her what they were doing with it and that it was okay. With that, she laid her head down and went to sleep. I then shared our exchange with her family, which opened a door for them to communicate with her in a new way while helping her work with her highly sensitive hearing and feeling abilities.

Two months later, a new client – the mother of a former co-worker – approached me. She had two dogs, one senior and one quite young, and a cat of her own, as well as the dog of her adult daughter, who was living in her home. I was brought in to do Reiki with her elder dog, as she had lost a canine contemporary in the previous six months and was not adjusting well to the loss. The younger dog could not understand her, and their energy levels were vastly different too.

The mom was also struggling. "It is not time," she said.

Much later, this phrasing, along with *I am not ready,* would become a subconscious tell on the parents' part. Though they did not realize they were sharing this, it spoke volumes about where each saw their pet on the life journey and, at the same time, their lack of acceptance of that reality. During these visits it was as much about holding space for the parents and sibling pets as it was for the elder or the one who was ill.

As I began working with this sweet elder, love and compassion opened my heart and allowed me to share these ideals by gently rubbing my hand against her front legs and paws – just as I would hold the hands of a revered grandmother. In fact, she reminded me of a grandmother in energy, age, and even in her love for lemon-flavored cookies, a likeness to my own maternal grandmother. Periodically, the younger sibling would just watch curiously. After I had been doing these Reiki sessions three times a week for a few weeks, the elder began eating more and putting on weight. The heavy, dense feeling in the home seemed to lighten as well. We grew quite close, and I felt I was getting a gift through my relationship with her on many levels of love.

A month later, I was scheduled for visits with the elder, the cat, and the daughter's dog, while the humans took the younger greyhound to a special weekend event. When I showed up to get the keys, the mom told me that the week before the elder had some stomach issues. She also said she thought that the dog had recovered, but left it to me to decide whether to do the visits; otherwise, she would stay home. I agreed to watch them as planned as it felt important on some unknown level.

The first several visits went as normal, but then things began to shift slightly. Unusual signs began showing up while I was driving to or from the house. We often in the beginning label these items as "coincidences" or just oddities in the scheme of everyday life. Yet, as I began acknowledging the occurrence and trying to discern the meaning, more messages appeared. I didn't always understand where they were heading, and sometimes I became so focused on one way of looking at them that I blocked myself off to other meanings.

On the way home from a visit one day, a large, older white car with a purple heart license plate did a U-turn in the middle of moving traffic, landing right in front of my car! Startled and scared, I slammed on my breaks while glancing in the rearview mirror to make sure I wasn't going to get hit from behind. What the message was, I didn't know, though I felt there was one. On another drive, a bunch of birds barely missed hitting my car, and at a third visit I asked the female cat how her sister was doing and she touched her paw to my heart. (In that moment, I saw the gesture as being separate from the question, as I was learning how quickly the animal beings respond.)

All of these were in the early stages of discernment and learning. It was like I was receiving page one of the textbook for Understanding Messages from Spirit, not always recognizing what the definitions were because I was so deeply involved in the details and emotions of their life experiences. I had trouble detaching myself from the day-to-day moments and shifting to the bigger picture that was playing out on her life stage.

Then one day I observed that while she was eating the others were only drinking water, which I thought was unusual. When the elder stopped taking her medicine – and refused to eat anything including her favorite lemon cookies – the others began eating. This was also on a day when neither the veterinarian office nor an emergency/urgent care office was open…the one day they were not open was the day things began shifting. It was like there was a higher power at work in the timing of this situation. The sibling and cousin seemed to recognize that she was entering another stage of her journey and, in hindsight, I realize they were showing deference to and holding space for her. When we went outside for the evening, we found it was relatively still, yet somehow the windchimes were really singing. I recorded it as it felt like something monumental was occurring, but since I'd never had such an experience with windchimes I wasn't sure what that something might be. Looking back, I realize this was a sign of future experiences when animal beings came in or let me know they were around in some way.

As she went around the yard, it felt different from how she typically did so. Somehow, this time was special, like she was going around the yard in gratitude, giving extra attention to each area and what it had provided: the scents, the sounds, and the experiences she'd had with the family there. There were no places open on a Sunday night to call to ask about what was going on; I noticed just how exhausted I felt during that last evening visit with her. It would take me seven years to realize that I was feeling how tired she was of living her life – feeling others' stuff, both animals and people, on an energetic level as well as a physical one. Indeed, it wasn't until recent years that I realized that sharing their energy is another way they communicate with us. Recognizing that it isn't mine, and understanding who it belongs to, is something I am still working to process and identify more quickly. I have learned it is important to ask my body, *Is this mine?* – another hard-won lesson as I had to first develop that kind of relationship with my body.

The following morning her mom took her to the doctor and learned she had congestive heart failure. Her sister was correct, as was the message from the car, with the heart on its license plate, that made a U-turn in front of me. They were bringing someone out to the house to put her to sleep and I asked if it was okay for me to be there. When I arrived, I offered her love and thanked her for the opportunity to support her the best I could at the time with a lot of unknowns on the table.

Though I had suffered a great deal of loss, this was the first time I had seen anyone – animal or human – transition. There was an emptiness I cannot explain, and when the mom wanted to record the experience for herself with a picture with the younger sister – the emotional pain that was evident in the younger sister's eyes could be felt deep within my heart. The mom didn't understand how the pets felt, knowing that the elder was no longer there and yet being asked to have a photo taken.

At that time I often felt it was crossing a line to say what I was picking up in the moment; I didn't know how or what to share. What came through later was, *If you were asked to have a photo taken with a loved one that just passed, how would you feel? Well, this is how the younger sister felt, and she was more aware than us of the exact moment the elder's soul left her physical body.* Of course, the mom did not do this intentionally; it was just something she did with each pet's passing, without considering the perspective of the other animal beings.

A month later, I visited with the crew and learned the cat had transitioned as well. It felt like the end of an era, with the elders passing the baton to the younger siblings as caretakers of their people. A few days after her passing, I had a dream visitation from her in which she appeared as a kitten, jumping up to sit on the laps of Jesus and Mother Mary before briefly showing herself atop the refrigerator. This was a message for her family – one I happily shared – that she would watch over them from her favorite spot.

It was challenging for me to experience these two passings within such a short time, similar to when I endured all the human deaths one after another, with only short periods of calm in between. Yet, I also knew it was a blessing to be there in support of the pets' journeys, as well as those of relatives. Much later, I began to see it as *traveling* with the being to wherever life took them next and being grateful for them choosing me to play a supporting role in their lives.

Many other lessons came a month later, when I was asked to care for the pets of two clients in a subdivision who were traveling together for sixteen days. Each had two dogs and both invited me to stay at their homes. I felt torn and chose to go with the person setting up the arrangements, rather than what would truly be best for me. This taught me that what one observes during a meet-and-greet holds more truth than what is being said (or not) and the importance of red flags, as well as not getting caught up in hearsay about what people in a neighborhood will or will not pay. I was new and undercharged for the assignment, which would be an ongoing lesson throughout the first several years regarding seeing and honoring my own value.

Some of the lessons had to do with what questions to ask with respect to the dogs in whose house I stayed overnight, as well as the pet parents' typical schedule. The lack of upfront information became evident when the dogs had accidents, regardless of how long I was there or even if I had just taken them outside. This was one level of exhaustion, and red flag number one. There had been an accident the day of the meet-and-greet, which I had inquired about and was told it was due to length of time the parent was away, but given there was newspapers laying in various spots on the floor I later questioned that answer and, as I said, was a test in observations and red flags in the form of parents' responses. Follow-up questions are key. There is a huge difference between a pet truly having an accident due to youth, aging, illness, or a longer wait for access to the outside versus a lack of training or "acting out" on their part – and you can feel the distinction.

These same two barked all night, every night, which meant there was very little sleeping on my part. I was getting an early education in what boundaries I needed to put in place to honor my sleep and health – and health was the most important, deep-level reason I had gone into business for myself. Yes, my love of animals is the reason I chose this type of business, but my health and the freedom to choose the components that would benefit my body, mind, emotions, and spirit were the key.

Now, it is not as easy as it sounds to honor yourself – this is what I learned as I butted up against my own personal beliefs, those of family, or societal norms. The only one who is going to keep your health at the top of the priority list is you; however, when you're a solopreneur there is no business if you are injured or sick. To get it right, I must continually choose what works for me long-term. This is why I quickly learned that I had to determine a cap for the number of overnights in a row, as well as the number of total pet visits per assignment or per day. It would take six years to pin down some of these numbers, knowing that even that could change depending on where life took me and where my energy levels were. Essentially, the Universe was drilling down on what was best for me and my business – and that included not comparing myself to what others can do. What I learned for myself with this assignment was to listen to my observations, the red flags, and that sleep is integral to sustainability, as well as my health.

This third assignment also taught me about seeing the pets beyond the situation – this was before I began recognizing that I was feeling and sensing everybody's emotions and physical stuff, including that of the animal beings, as my own. Looking back, I was most likely picking up on the frustration and emotions of the dogs whose home I was staying in, which made the situation inherently more challenging. In the other friend's household, I met a sweet, lovable fourteen-year-old and his brother, who was half his age. The elder gentleman, I was told, had stopped going for walks, and if he did go out he would stop by the mailbox less than fifty feet away and refuse to go any further. As a result, his mom had stopped taking him when she went out with his brother or when they joined the neighbor. My mother knew the woman, so I asked if she would be willing to be the younger brother's walking companion while we all went for a jaunt around the block to a small doggy park, and she agreed. I could then see if the elder would like to go with us.

After suiting up the younger brother, I went into the laundry area to get the elder's leash. When he saw it, he started dancing from one paw to the other as he realized he was being asked to go along with his brother. I looked him in the eyes and told him, "You get to decide the pace and how far you want to go…it is entirely up to you." And as we headed out towards the mailbox, I thought, *This will be interesting.* He literally ran past it, and he continued along the sidewalk, taking in all the scents and sights. We stopped at the halfway point, which was the dog park, for him to rest and for all to enjoy the light breeze and pretty spring day. After a while, we started toward home, with him walking a bit slower. His brother, who led the pack with my mom, would drop back periodically to check in on him and make sure he was okay.

When we returned to the house, the elder's eyes were brighter and, though he was tired from the walk, he was happy and his energy was lighter. We did this a few more times every couple of days. The elders cannot always keep the same pace as they once did, nor can they often do so every day – yet it doesn't always mean *not ever again.* Sometimes all it takes is someone new who did not know them as they were before, to see and accept them as they are – and understand what they enjoy doing now. We spent many days sitting out in the shade on his back patio as I connected with them during my visits.

Six months later, I awakened to a dream with the elder. I saw the mailbox as confirmation of who was coming through, then an upstairs, which always depicts a higher level of consciousness, followed by the elder laying across the threshold of the back sliding glass door. A day later, I received a call from his mother that he had crossed the Rainbow Bridge the day before, which was shared in the dream as he crossed the threshold from one realm to the next.

This threshold would become a message many additional pet kids would use to share that they were crossing or getting closer to the final stage. Some would have accidents, typically pooping at the threshold from one room to the next to share they were preparing or ready to release their physical bodies – a lesson for me that they are often ready before we are. Others would show it by sitting at the edge of a lit room, signifying that they were moving to the light or to what many call heaven or the Rainbow Bridge.

In June of that first year, I met another elder in the form of a miniature schnauzer, who was the first I found to enjoy being read to during our visits together. We would sit next to each other, with him appearing to be napping as I read. At some point, a paw would be gently laid upon my knee, which I eventually realized was his way of telling me to pay particular attention to something in whatever book I was reading. He didn't move his paw until the content and how it related to me was understood. As I connected with him and opened my heart more, we found lots of love and support for one another.

For me, books, both fiction and non-fiction, always contain messages or examples of lessons I am working on at any given time. The fact that he stopped me gently for each of these taught me that animal beings are listening, understanding, and have a lot more to contribute and offer us daily as we work through our lives. When we open the door and acknowledge what we are receiving, we then can provide a channel for it to show up more. In my experience, there are many ways, almost akin to different languages or dialects, in which animal beings bring messages through, though each has their own unique style. If you are a pet parent, your furbabies likely have one or two key ways they communicate with you.

Nearly a year later, this sweet guy crossed the Rainbow Bridge after several falls into the family swimming pool. Pools are often a message of renewal, so falling in multiple times is a sign of things to come. Then he began circling, which is a form of late-stage canine dementia. When I was asked to do Reiki with him and see what I got, he circled the entire time until I asked if he was ready to depart. It was then that he stopped the circling before beginning once again. The message: departing is the only thing that will stop the circling or the progress of the disorder, and I am ready for it to stop. What also came through while being with him was that he wanted to know if it was okay for him to move on from his family, as he had assisted them through a tough illness. He was looking for consent.

In July of this first year, I met the family of two golden retrievers – an older female and a male puppy – who were in my life for about seven months until they moved out of town. The puppy was finding his way on his new life journey. His big sister was a wonderful teacher who would let him discover his path and then guide him along with her special type of mentoring. There were times he was relentless in some of his puppy stages as for him everything was about fun, curiosity, and play!

The more play and fun, the happier the kid was, but so too was his energy wound up. She, on the other hand, sometimes wanted to just chill in the yard, and so we would sit on the grass together while each got their needs met. She loved Reiki and receiving love through our connection, as well as from a like-minded contemporary of sorts.

We were all learning to communicate and understand each other in our different styles of speaking in verbal, non-verbal, and intuitive messages. I always knew when they received the message that something one or the other had shared was understood by me, because when I arrived the next time there was the greeting, as well as a special celebration. They were big teachers of the concept that every step, regardless of how big or small it seemed, was meant to be celebrated – and an ongoing reminder to me and all of us who are experiencing life at this time.

The kid was still in a crate, which helped the older sister as it gave her some downtime from the hustle and bustle of life with a toddler. His crate was divided into two sections, one with a puppy pad and the other with his bed, with a gate of sorts in the middle. He began shredding the puppy pads, yet they were always dry. One day I asked him why and he proceeded to show me by going in through the main crate door and contorting his body to get himself through the gate into the bed area. He was showing through his form of communication that he was getting too big to have the areas separated and no longer needed the puppy pads. I told him I would share his message with his dad and the next day when I arrived a celebration ensued as his crate was now one big space!

One day, when we were all outside together, the kid and I were standing near one another while sis stood just slightly beyond my left shoulder on the patio. Suddenly, some birds flew into the yard, and *I heard* in a high-pitched cartoon, kid-like voice, "Look at that, isn't that cool!" I knew in my soul it was coming from the younger brother. At the same time, out of the corner of my left eye I saw his sister just barely making a methodical, extremely slow movement with her back right leg. Then I heard the kid-like voice say, "Oh that's right, this is my yard," as he raced to chase them out barking the whole time! Yes, we are all learning – and there were times when the sister's heightened level of patience came through as a teacher. For me, hearing animal beings like that was one I hoped to experience more frequently.

Chapter Eleven

NO TWO RESPOND THE SAME

*I*n mid-August I met an apprehensive senior Jack Russell terrier who wasn't fond of young kids and other pets, especially cats. The rescue shelter believed he was nine years old when the parents adopted him. The first time I saw him with one of the parent's granddaughters, I noticed she was forcibly trying to move his face to scratch his neck. I read his body language, then shared with her and with her parent that he didn't want to be touched in that manner. He didn't like his face pulled up. I then put it into language that may be understood by saying, "Would you want someone coming up to you and pulling your face like that?" I could see she was thinking it over as the pup moved closer to me. I learned she also had a dog, but some of it is educating that, just as no two people respond the same way, neither do pets – and to expect that is setting both parties up for failure.

I found that he loved to do anything together, but his style of fetch came with a caveat: you had to be willing to play as well. What this meant is he would fetch the ball and drop it half-way between us so that I could run and get it. In our early visits we would sit outside watching the sunset in between bouts of play, then head inside for a brushing session that lasted as long as he wished.

He did not like the television or cellphone when I visited as he saw those as distractions and he had spent most of his day away from those he loved. The first and only time I did so, he immediately went outside to talk to the neighbors through his communication method of *barking*. It all stopped when the electronics disappeared and I played games, connected soulfully with him, or brushed him. Sometimes I read a bit at night, which was okay if he was ready for bed; the rest of the time was spent enjoying each other's company. What I discovered over time was this was the best gift I could give those pets I stayed or visited with: the gift of undeniable presence.

It was in these moments – whether inside, playing, loving on them with a brush or otherwise, or going for a walk without being connected to the phone – that I showed I was choosing to be with them in the way they connect with others: fully giving of themselves. The more you can let your hair down, so to speak, with them and be in a status of joy, the more connected you will be. This is an ongoing lesson the animal beings and pet friends are teaching us. And yes, just like you I am still *human* – meaning I occasionally fall out of this space. When this happens I quickly feel the animal being's disgruntled energy, which can also look like "Fine, I will go into another room then."

Two weeks after this assignment, I would find myself riding a rollercoaster of emotions regarding my dad's health. Mom and I – as well as Dad, of course – lived in a constant state of stress not knowing where these experiences were taking us. It was also challenging not knowing how much and how often to share with my brother, especially since Dad could go from being on the mend (or seeming so) to being on a downward spiral within the same day – sometimes within the same hour. He had fallen while walking up and down the hallway of my parents' building, which was how he got his three-plus miles of exercise each day. It hadn't always been this way. My parents had always enjoyed walks together; however, the two-heart related incidents Dad had suffered while on these walks, and the anxiety they ignited in him, had robbed them of that activity.

His fall in the hallway had resulted in a fractured pelvis and landed him in the emergency room, followed by admittance to the hospital and a two-week stay in a rehab center. During those two weeks it became evident that my maternal grandmother in spirit was helping him from the other side, as each and every day he wanted his bedside table set up a specific way – with the exact placement, down to the inch, that we had once seen with her. Plus, during this stay and only this one, he wanted ginger ale, which – you guessed it – was my grandmother's go-to beverage.

Shortly after Dad got out, the three of us took my nephew, who was thirteen at the time, to several places in California while his parents went on a trip. I was grateful for the lighter experience. We began to realize just how important getaways were to our mental and emotional health – though this was something I had already been learning from my pet friends. They brought love, new perspectives, friendship, and an opportunity to get into a much lighter space through play and focusing on their own levels of joy. They helped me shift from worry and denser energy patterns and situations to a higher vantage point from which to view life.

For more than six years the Jack Russell had been one of my overnight buddies, as well as one of my greatest teachers (I'd say he learned from my teachings as well). We had helped each other work through our various insecurities, and he had also helped me see situations with my dad's health in a new light. He even stepped past some of the things we had been told he disliked in order to *teach me*.

In the summer months, he'd want to go to sleep around 8:30 in the evening and go out for a walk around 4 a.m., so I would quickly get on his schedule, which allowed for a beautiful, long walk before the Arizona heat kicked up. One day, we started in the dark, which somewhat unnerved me in unknown territories, in part because it triggered the thought that someone might jump out at me from the darkness (a teaching from my youth).

He proceeded to show me that friends were all around by periodically stopping and staring at an area until I followed his gaze to whatever feline was hidden in the spots. Twelve hidden felines made themselves be seen by us by briefly moving into lit areas, walking beside us, or allowing their presence to be known or felt through energy that morning. This reminded me of stories relatives had told me of my maternal great-grandmother feeding the homeless, both human and animal. I knew that this woman, whom I had never met, was walking with us that morning.

Growing up, I was always wary of people but had a natural love and respect for the animal beings. Now my canine friend, as well as the felines and my great-grandmother, were sharing that not everyone we come across in the dark or an unknown area is out to get us. We can share love and respect for the other beings on our paths who, just like us, are doing their best to be accepted and seen for who they are.

My pup friend took this a step further, and beyond his comfort zone, to help another who had gotten separated from his family. One morning, a young German Shepherd started following us as we walked around the local elementary school. It took me a few minutes to realize that my dog friend was allowing him to do so without a bark of any kind. Once that was understood, I stopped and began softly speaking to the pup and discovered he didn't have any identification on. Wondering how we were going to locate his family, I asked my spiritual guides for help. That is when others in the community, who were walking past with their own dogs, stopped to say that his family was looking for him. We stayed by the school until, sure enough, we saw an extended cab pickup with a family roll to a stop as they called out their boy's name. After briefly looking at us as if thanking us, he ran toward his people, and my friend and I made our way back to the house.

In later years, things would begin to change for my friend as his eyesight and depth perception began to diminish. Things he used to love doing became a bit more challenging, including some types of play and being outside as the light decreased and the sun set into darkness. Whereas before he would stay out, he seemed anxious and agitated at this time of day – similar to the sundowner's syndrome that some people experience.

This also showed up during our early-morning adventures, when he would start walking toward vehicle lights, not recognizing them as something to stay away from. In hindsight, I realize that he was walking toward the light. When I stayed overnight he often slept up beside me or at the foot of the bed, then periodically got down to go outside but was not able to see to get back up. I would awake, sense him standing nearby, and wrap my arms around him, telling him that on the count of three I would pick him up. This would happen a few times before we both went into a deep sleep.

Around the same time I met a sweet, middle-aged, red-haired female dog – one of the first animal beings to send me dream messages during our overnight experiences. She too loved integrated interactions, LOVED her walks, playing hide-and-seek, with her toys, and swimming together, as well as getting ten minutes of mid-morning sun to soak in the vitamin D she needed. She helped me get into a kid-like play space even more – something I thought I had lost long ago. We played a story-like game that pushed me to do some new things I typically would not have done around people. I provided voices for her toys, and this started a new process of play with others who came into the business.

I helped her through some of her insecurities around fireworks, thunderstorms, and changes that were taking place for her as well as in her family. Likewise, she helped me with messages from loved ones in spirit and others (known and unknown) who were coming through my dreams more and more. One, oddly enough, was David Bowie, who taught me that it was okay to be different, to be uniquely me – and the importance of accepting who I was and sharing that with others. I would often get messages while at various classes, two of which were equine therapy-based classes where an oracle card could be pulled. In both cases the card was that of a zebra, which provides a similar message of being boldly you as each zebra has a unique to them pattern of stripes, like a fingerprint.

The red-haired lady and I had many special moments during our five years together. One of her favorite things was pushing me outside my comfort zone by indicating, during our walks, specific people for me to stop and speak with. These people needed special connection – and my friend was well aware that had they been animal beings I'd have been there in a heartbeat. Doing so with humans was not in my wheelhouse; however, people with pet friends were more receptive to impromptu conversation, as the animal beings naturally broke the ice. I wasn't always at ease with permitting the interaction, depending on the client, the pet, and what my anxieties were in connection with the people; however, these experiences were her joyful moments. I was learning that each animal friend was a teacher of some concept or life lesson, and each brought about amazing relationships. These experiences are often solely thought of with our human counterparts – however, these can occur with any *living being* when one opens the door.

We had a lot of fun and blessed moments on our journey together – sitting in a corner of her yard overlooking the open space; following her specially-guided walks when she always showed me a new route to her favorite park or the school where she loved watching the kids play; or enjoying quiet moments inside together or walking through the storms that appear in our lives and discovering ways to enjoy the rain that washes over us. There was such love and humor in her eyes when she looked at me or when she snuck in kisses as I tried to get a selfie with her. Just before the pandemic lockdown occurred, we were together and there was just something different going on that I could not explain at the time. Everything we see is based on the lens we look through, so if our lens is focused on one thing we can miss something entirely different. All I knew is that something was unusual about this time with her, and I questioned it even further when I heard myself sharing how much I loved getting to know her, thanking her for all the lessons she taught me, opening herself to allow me into her life, and offering her gratitude for our special relationship. I realized in that moment I was fully present with her as an observer of us both on a different plane of existence – one that would be fully understood six short months later when she crossed the Rainbow Bridge.

Walking the journey with my dad helped me open up and communicate what I was feeling with my animal friends even more; it also facilitated greater access to the meaningful shared experiences with each of these beings. As with the people in our lives, we have a limited amount of precious time with these beautiful beings; therefore, I felt it important that they knew they were loved and that I was grateful for our time together.

Sometimes it would take me several minutes to leave as I told them how much I loved them, and how grateful I was for their friendship and the opportunity to spend time with them. They all know that the final time I say it is after I get in my vehicle, and I am pulling away from their home. Yes, we have all learned that life can be short on this physical plane. I also know that they are very much open to connection with us from the other side. Know that they are only a heartbeat away, and in the moment you think about them, recall a memory, say their name, or feel them in your heart, they are with you.

Chapter Twelve

CONNECTIONS AND SYNCHRONICITY

One day, after returning from a visit with my brother and his family in Texas, I received a phone call from someone saying that a friend of theirs who had moved to Texas found my website and thought I would be a good one to reach out to regarding visits with her pets. Most of my clients already knew me, or found me through referrals or social media, while many others, such as this one, came to me in synchronistic, even otherworldly ways. One example was one pet family moving away, only to have another that lived on the same street, several miles away and in another neighborhood to find me.

In this situation, a dog had torn some ligaments in her knees while out playing in the yard with her rabbit sibling – they loved playing tag and following their joy with one another. After agreeing and setting up a meet-and-greet, I got off the phone. When I tuned into the two animal beings, I saw the rabbit near a sliding glass door and learned that she was worried about her friend thinking she had hurt her in some way through their play. I reassured her through my heart and mind that it was no one's fault.

When I arrived, the dog was happy to see me and wanted me to go outside to see where her friend lived. She started toward a sliding glass door. There was a feeling of just knowing that both had received my message and knew I had received theirs.

During my first visits with them, whenever I asked if they were open to Reiki, the pup would guide me outside to sit where her friend was so both could connect and receive. With time, the timid rabbit came out to be seen and, by the end of our first pet-sitting assignment, she would tap me on the foot as a way to say thanks for allowing her to choose the level and pace of our engagement. There was a camaraderie among us as friends and beings who understood one another.

In subsequent visits, we would continue to learn more about one another's joys in our interactions through companionship, mealtime, lunch time snacks, play, and the Reiki, which continued. I was learning that the dog was okay with her sister visiting with me *after* she had her one-on-one time with me during our first visit of each assignment. Once we were past that point, all were okay sharing my love and connection. I recognized that my pup friend enjoyed companionship while she ate and in fact would only eat when I was sitting nearby, which reminded me of my "early Arizona" buddy. It's all about love and sharing it with them. Her rabbit sister began opening more with me by sitting next to me on the patio floor, followed by coming up behind me to tap me on the back in a "guess who" type of play before racing off, only to come back later during our early mornings or night-time visits.

A year or so ago, my rabbit friend passed and my canine friend and I have worked to find a new rhythm during our visits. She occasionally goes over to the area where her sibling hung out during the day to share that her buddy-in-spirit is visiting or that she misses her and their companionship. She and I enjoy sitting together outside and listening to the morning awaken or the yard going to sleep in peaceful connection. She has always been a clear channel for messages to come through, sometimes about what we are doing, other times about an incoming phone call or request for me and what will happen if I agree to it. Unfortunately, my learning hasn't always been as quick, so some of the messages I learned the hard way by running around picking up keys in order to fit a client visit into my packed day instead of thinking it through to determine if that saying yes meant saying no to taking in nourishment for my body. She also has been helping me learn more about myself and that for many of these beautiful and gentle beings I am a channel to feel, hear, or sense their love, connection, or messages.

She was there when chiropractic treatments began last year, bringing my spinal cord back on board in its communications. She taught me that as it was rebooted, I would begin to hear and feel things differently, and that my senses would heighten so things would sound louder or I would be more in tune with higher levels of energy – all of which has indeed been the case over the last several months. The access channel to my emotions also seems to be more open as well and the tears just appear on the surface where previously they remained hidden. When it happened with her one day, she laid her paw gently on my arm in a gesture of love and compassion, letting me know she understood what was happening. Smells appear stronger, radios and sounds louder, lights now appear brighter, I get tired more quickly by being around lots of people and when entering a home where something emotional took place at some point before my arrival (arguments, grieving, or heavy discussions). Each of these results in a need to get out to connect with the healing environment and energy of nature to ground and center myself.

Last year, she sent me messages as I was traveling to her house to teach me that my receptor was not only back online, but heightening. I always visualize the pets that I will be visiting with next as I leave my place or a prior client's house to let them know I am on my way, and I can feel when the message has been received. I can also tell when I am not fully present as I do not get a clear connection – it's like getting static on a cell phone when we are out of the service area. That day, I definitely got evidence that my receiver was increasing because I felt her message that she was hungry with my own stomach suddenly ravenous and growling! I knew it was her because I had not been hungry at all beforehand and I saw her face pop up in my mind's eye. I acknowledged her message, saying I was three lights away and would get her breakfast as soon as I arrived. I felt her receive it and, with that, I was no longer hungry.

They all teach, accept, and have a reciprocal relationship with us when we are open to the magic all around us and what is possible with these beings of love and light. She is one of the first who accepted hugs and offered her own side hug version as well. Just thinking about these moments with her, our hugs, and the love we share brings joy to my heart, and a large smile to my face. It fills me up with the light of love.

My maternal grandmother and dad continued to share a thread of similar situations in their later years together. It brought to my mind questions about who was projecting and who was absorbing emotions, physical experiences, or if both were experiencing a life lesson where one showed one aspect and the other offered mirrored responses to the lesson. It was difficult at times to step back from the details and the emotions to truly see what was unfolding. As I mentioned previously, in one such situation, my father ended up in the same hospital room as my grandmother the very day she was discharged.

Another time, both ended up needing shots for their back issues – and you guessed it – on the same day during the same appointment time. I was grateful during those first several years for the lighter schedule so I could be there for my parents through each shift that occurred. On the other hand, it did affect how quickly (or slowly) my business grew. So much of my emotional and physical energy was devoted to helping them, though I did my best to achieve balance by bringing my laptop with me to work on some of the administration tasks wherever I was.

I have noticed over the past six months that my mom and I are doing our own similar dance. In December, I had challenges and required her assistance; in January, she had surgery and needed my help for the next several months. I then had health and eye tests, followed by her getting them – all reminders that we all need help at various times in our lives.

Mom and I have noticed certain twin-like mindsets, lessons in relationships, and even similar health things appearing. It took a while before we realized that we were actually tapping into one another's thoughts! We still are not sure which of us initiates the thought, but we both end up having a part in it. For instance, she gets out of the car to take a package to the UPS store. I say in her absence, *I need to get her phone out to open an app for a coffee shop since we are stopping there for breakfast (*something she had often asked of me in the past),* only to hear when she returns that she was thinking the same thing. It's happened with what's for dinner, shopping ideas, what we are wearing, and the like.

I met a family of five pups – the result of one having a bum knee and needing some calming love and compassion. Over the next couple of months we enjoyed getting to know one another, and I noticed that some in this crew communicated with me in different ways than others. The four boys in the family were more demonstrative in showing what they wanted or what they were talking about with me; moreover, two of them were more reserved or insecure in the beginning while the sister was more outgoing, friendly, and often the leader of the pack when it came to requesting t-r-e-a-t-s.

Whatever their differences, I quickly found that they all loved Reiki. Each family has their own patterns in terms of what we do together and how each interacts with each other in my presence, as well as how they interact with me. The eldest male of this crew was teaching the more skittish one, who would observe his older brother's relating with me and my response, allowing him to slowly begin to open to me. The elder brother loved to receive hands-on Reiki while showing his love for our connection and relationship. There was an understanding between us. It was after the elder's passing that my somewhat skittish friend freely began to step outside his comfort zone and jump up on my lap and share kisses, as well as a deeper connection with me.

They helped me share changes I was witnessing in the other members of the family – not just the typical alpha/subordinate dynamic, but where they each were in their journey. The sweet elder sister transitioned just before Halloween last year, showing in various ways that she was ready to release her physical body for ease of movement. The following weekend I took the boys for a walk, a new experience for the four of us – this, after giving us a day together to honor their sister's legacy and our love as a group.

During our first walk together, we saw three dogs that looked exactly like their sister – a message that wherever they and the parents were she would always be just a few steps beyond them. There was such a feeling of warmth and love during the walk and our additional visits together that I know in my heart and soul she was with us. Six short months later, her previously skittish brother would follow in her footsteps across the Rainbow Bridge not long after a new pup friend joined the pack – an exuberant and loving presence doing her best to bring an element of play and joy to lift everyone out of their sadness. I have the pleasure of still visiting with this crew and look forward to our explorations together.

Chapter Thirteen

THE RISE AND FALL OF THE WATER

*I*n 2017, we experienced extreme lows and great highs when it came to my dad's health. He began retaining lots of fluid in his abdomen, which required several trips to the hospital to drain it. The three of us hit an all-time low – mentally, physically, and emotionally – when, after draining seventeen pounds (7.7 liters of fluid) the medical staff told us it was time for him to go on hospice. I went through some deep emotional clearing by going through pictures of Dad and recalling all the experiences I had with him, from childhood to working together at the college in Georgia. It was a very challenging time.

An aunt visited for a weekend to help shift our focus, after which I was scheduled to leave on a cruise with a friend. For the first time during the roller-coaster with my dad's health, I reached out to my brother to ask him to come from out of town to support our parents while I was away. This was very difficult, both in terms of asking for assistance and the trip itself, as I was putting my own needs ahead of theirs for the first time. It was only after my brother agreed to come that I felt a bit more comfortable in moving forward with my plans.

I had my own ups and downs throughout the cruise, working to stay out of worry about what may be happening at home. I was several days in before I was able to move beyond the energy of the previous weeks. It helped that the trip had structure, as it was a combination of education and recreation. Interestingly, my phone would not receive calls from home, nor would it work with the ship's system that allowed participants of the program to connect. In essence, Spirit was telling me to trust the process. I was where I was meant to be, as hard as that was.

During that trip I met two guys who looked and felt energetically like loved ones in spirit, so much so that I felt as though I was hanging out with my relatives again. I also had an experience with a great-uncle, who died before my dad was born but came through during a journaling experience. There were lots of messages supporting my steps to get there. One of the activities a friend and I did was two-person kayaking in the open water, which was challenging. In hindsight, it was a great metaphor for how Spirit can be directing and supporting you on your journey, but we cannot always see the ways they are helping us. This trip pushed me in many ways beyond what I would have done had I been home.

Upon my return, I was relieved to see that my dad was starting to overcome the depression he had been in since the doctor's diagnosis. Pivotal in this process was a collection of

DVDs from "The Great Courses," given to him by my aunt (who had visited with us before my trip) and uncle. As the name suggests, The Great Courses was a series of class lectures, and Dad, a lifelong learner and former collegiate professor, was immediately hooked, especially on the science courses, as he had taught chemistry and others. The Great Courses allowed him to shift away from worry and into a cycle of healing as he turned off his usual triggering news-related programming to things that reminded him of his joy of teaching.

During this time he was still retaining fluid in his abdomen as a side effect of the heart issues. His weight was constantly monitored, and when the scale climbed to a specific number he would have to go for a paracentesis – an outpatient procedure in which a needle was inserted to drain the fluid. To put this into perspective, he'd go through some similar symptoms to pregnant women: changes in his body put pressure on his sciatic nerve, causing numbness in a leg or balance issues and falls, depending on how much fluid had accumulated over each two- to three-week period. Yet, despite these ongoing physical challenges, his mindset was in a much better space, which contributed to his healing.

I now realize that during this challenging time I was learning how to take risks and step further outside my comfort zone – asking my brother for assistance and stepping forward with the cruise – which would assist me in the coming years with other challenges. There was also an ongoing lesson playing out in my dad's life experience – one that originated with his mom's passing while he was on vacation. Later trips planned and agreed upon by him would eventually deteriorate as apprehension or worry entered his mindset and a health situation occurred, resulting in cancellations. Now we might understand this as an emotional trauma, wound, or block playing out each time a set of specific elements is in play.

I observed my mom as the primary caretaker struggling with each delay; for her, these trips were a way to shift focus, access her joy, and learn new things. I also found it challenging to get excited about events; each time, I would hope it would be "all systems go," but rarely did it pan out. Sometimes we would get closer, only to be stopped once again a few short days before. Yet, despite the constant feeling of being at a standstill, we were actually moving forward, albeit in hidden and unrecognized ways.

This pattern of events would show up in other ways in our lives, including in my business; I would get really excited by a new idea, only for the energy to shift and a block or wall to rise up before me. It has taken quite a while to begin unraveling where this formula originated and how it entered my life and business environment. It is often easier to see the big picture and lessons in reflection or, at times, through another person's journey than it is when we are going through the process.

In each of these experiences, we may have actually been closer than we thought to the destination (trip, project, or other), yet it can feel like a hundred if our ego or our own firewalls come into play, spouting all our insecurities like mantras to stop us from crossing that final bridge to the destination. At the same time, we must strain to hear the soft-spoken voice within that is working up the courage to be heard once and for all, asking us to release the burdens and beliefs of our past. These burdens and beliefs hold us in a stationary or circling pattern, like pigeons taking flight only to land in the exact spot they vacated a few minutes earlier. That soft voice is working to dismantle the blocks so we can see components in a new way, rewrite the code for how to live, and grasp the new, healthier life we have been on the path to since starting this journey.

People would tell me that, in their opinion, my steps or actions were making my path harder than it needed to be. However, the important thing to remember is that each of us is built differently. No two people process, see, feel, and understand things in exactly the same way, so what is perceived as easy or hard to one will be different from another. At that point in my life, I needed to understand why the actions I was taking or not resulted in the outcome I desired. I needed to find that missing piece to move beyond the self-imposed insecurities that my overthinking created. I realized that these insecurities were often built on illusion and therefore easily knocked down once we acknowledge them and continue taking steps forward; however, just as parenting doesn't come with a handbook or a link to a video, neither did this process.

This is the same for any new endeavor. How often do we stop the forward energy just before rolling it out or pressing the enter or submit buttons? I recognize that this has occurred in my business, working on this book (which was delayed several years), and other ideas in which there was too much worry that it wasn't the right time, I was not following the right path, or I wasn't listening to my intuition.

On the other hand, a pause was needed when it came to this book, for it allowed me to retrieve some of the key pieces. In fact, one of the things I learned while writing this book is that intuitive ideas must be coupled with inspired action – be it research, reaching out to someone to ask a question, or brainstorming a list of potential tasks that will take me to my goal. I also learned it was important to write out at the end of each day what I had accomplished, which was a game-changer in 2023 and far more valuable than putting together a to-do list and then chastising myself for what I didn't get to. Focusing on what I had done by the end of the day created more of that *completion* energy and brought forth the ability to follow through to the finish line.

Upon returning from the trip, I met two new animal friends in the form of two senior female canines, one tall and one short. They had other differences as well, and though their stories had some similar themes, their relationship was not necessarily a healthy one. I was the first non-family member to watch their pets.

Initial meet and greets give parents time to adjust to me, see how I am with their pets, and how I can build relationships with everyone moving forward. This was especially true with this family. The shorter of the two pups had landed in the home after the passing of one of the human's parents. The other was left there by an adult son, whose new living situation was not the best for a dog.

When I came into the household, I picked up that the adult child's dog felt lost as to how she ended up separated from her person wondering what she had done wrong; this situation was further exacerbated by the power struggles over toys, attention, and such between her and the other dog. One day her person dropped by while I was there, and when I told him she didn't understand he took the time to chat with her. She seemed much calmer after that – she needed to hear it directly from him.

Another day, I realized that these ladies had the power to connect through the dream state with me. In a dream, I saw two older *human* women who were sharing that I wouldn't be getting off at their exit. As I worked to figure out who the women were and thought I had identified them, I received a confirmation message in the form of a phone call from their mom saying there had been a change in plans for the day. You might wonder why they showed themselves in human form. What I have learned in my connection with animal friends is that it is based on how they see our relationship and how they know I treat them. I see them as equals and therefore when they can, or they have the ability, they show our relationship based on how it feels.

In some cases, it may be to teach a new concept. When I walk into a household it is normal to greet all the beings, human or otherwise, in the same manner, with the same amount of respect. Those who come into this life in an animal form are no less than those who come in as a human. All are beings that have special skill sets and abilities. I found the taller girl enjoyed the quiet moments spent together one-on-one receiving Reiki and being read to, while her smaller sister's love language was often action-based, which caused some early friction until we learned ways to incorporate both styles into our visits.

Six months later, the taller of the two girls passed away at home. It was sad and hard to see in such a short time, but I was blessed to have this wonderful opportunity to meet, get to know her, and help her find closure with her person while enjoying many fun and loving moments together.

This began a new phase with her sister, with us going on walks to shift up the energy in her household while also creating our own memories together. In the beginning, it was just around the block; then, with my support, she started venturing out of her comfort zone. There were times when she had some medical challenges that made walking difficult, so I would pick her up and carry her until she wanted down to check something out. When she had healed, she was ready to venture into new territory. Sometimes it was walking to a nearby elementary school and other times around several smaller subdivisions close by. She enjoyed seeing wildlife of all types and was even warming up to some of the school-age kids who wanted to stop and pet her – things she wasn't too sure about previously – but she discovered that they were curious about her and friendly. She was also teaching that we all can change when we are open to it.

During our walks, she faced several insecurities: large, monstrous trucks that were smelly and loud as they blew past us, knocking us off balance; landscaping crews with their loud equipment that caused vibrations that could be felt even inside the home; and thunderstorms, which were a huge foe. We explored grassy areas and fall leaves; we met geese, ducks, blue herons, and master egrets. We played inside games when it was too hot to be outside in the summer months, creating stories around her adventures so she and her family could see her bravery as we helped each other grow and change.

There were days she didn't want to return from our outings and was even willing to walk in sprinkles of rain (not a typical favorite for this girl) – changes that amazed and shocked her family. I remember how insecure I was about picking her up at the beginning of our visits, as my tremors were more prevalent at the time. Yet we built a strong relationship of trust in the aftermath of her sister's passing, and our walk on the anniversary of that day was one of memories and special times. Though they didn't always get along, there was a recognition of the journey together, a continual celebration of her sister's life.

Before long, a shift occurred within her family when the father retired, followed by a move. The timing was very synchronistic, for as they were exiting my life, my father's health situation began declining once again.

In the last quarter of 2017, two reserved feline brothers around the age of six came in. I learned that one was slightly more outgoing than his sibling, and their mom said not to worry if I did not see them. Apparently, no one else who had visited with the duo had either. One of the things I felt very strongly about was that all animal beings deserved time spent with them, whether they were seen or not. I saw this with many feline friends: you have to give the more reserved or insecure one a reason to come out. If you are going to be in and out in fifteen minutes, the likelihood of them being seen or for them to perceive the visit as being worth their time isn't good.

On the first visit with this crew, I didn't see anyone; then again, I had set off the alarm, so it would have been a major miracle if anyone ventured out after that! And yet, it kind of *cleared the air,* opening it up for a new beginning. The second day, the more adventurous of the two joined me after I took care of some tasks and he continued to visit with me each day of the assignment. He accepted some love and touch when I arrived in the kitchen. He enjoyed watching the birds in the yard and on the patio, so I would sit and watch them with him enjoying our time together. His brother wouldn't make an appearance during this first vacation assignment, though the drop-off and pickup of the key gave him a chance to connect with his safety net, in the form of his mom nearby.

The first visit of our second assignment together started with the outgoing one joining me right away, and ended with him sitting at the end of the hall during our playtime together. I ventured down and there sat his brother, sitting on the threshold between the hall and the bedroom he liked. One step more and he'd venture out of his comfort zone; for now, though, he appeared undecided as to whether he was ready. I sat down on the floor, giving him extra space and the three of us played games in the hallway for the remainder of the visit. I shared with him that his brother and I would love to have him join us during my visits and for the rest of the assignment he did just that… once all the tasks were done.

He continued to branch out more, facing his insecurities around people and noises. He always knew when someone was approaching the front door and he would zip down the hall to the safety of his room until the coast was clear. With time, patience, and love, he began staying out, even as shifts in the environment occurred. Both would start joining me in the kitchen, with this kid coming out after his brother had his time with me; then we would play before I took care of the daily tasks. With each assignment that followed he became more at ease with the experience, and, in recent years, he remained out in the front room to wait for my arrival, whether day or night. He had grown beyond his insecurities of those earlier times to truly trust and enjoy our friendship.

Chapter Fourteen

LESSONS IN LISTENING

No matter the animal – cat or dog, rabbit or turtle, guinea pig, red-eared slider turtle, painted turtle, bearded dragon, beta fish, lizard, and so on – all have the capacity to connect in some way. This goes for the wilder varieties as well.

I learned this first-hand when I met a young pup and his desert tortoise sister. The tortoise would teach me a lot about her own comprehension of what was going on with me, as well as the ways she and her brother communicated. If I didn't understand her message right away, the brother would explain in his own way, "translating" her request.

The pup loved to lay atop me like I was one of his pack, along with one of his stuffed toys; he also enjoyed running and playing in his yard. As the youngster grew up, we began going on walks together while understanding one another's communication styles more. Often when he was seemingly misbehaving there was a message he was trying to convey. Stepping away from the details to look at the big picture is key and I am learning to get to that stage sooner. Taking off with a glove that, from a higher vantage point, looked like a *hand* was his way of saying, *"I can handle it,"* or *"I have a handle on it."* Jumping into the swimming pool was often a message asking me to *go with the flow, keep swimming (keep moving forward), or jump on in (take the leap).*

He loved going for walks and learned that when we moved from the concrete to the grassy areas, I would run as fast as I could while laughing like a kid with him across the wide-open field. In his mind, this favorite activity only improved when the sprinklers surprised (and soaked) us. If you decide to do this, make sure your car keys are firmly secure in your bag or pocket as trying to locate them afterward is impossible! Yes, the lessons we learn can step outside the typical scope of the perceived work.

One fall day, his sister was trying to tell me something by walking under me. When the pup realized the message wasn't coming through, he proceeded to start digging. That is when I said, *"Oh, you want your hibernation spot created."* By walking under me, she was saying she wanted to go below the surface of the ground. At that moment, he stopped digging and laid down. I told them I would let their parents know that she was ready to start going in for the colder nights before it was time for full hibernation. As I acknowledged this request and their messages, she slowly put her foot atop his paw in gratitude. These sweet moments are beautiful – and one could easily miss them if not observing their actions or being a witness to their communication with one another. She would often share some leftover lettuce with him. Their love language with one another was that of service.

In the early days with his sister, she enjoyed walking around the yard with me while I chatted with her. Then we would meet up with her brother where he was enjoying his yard and the three of us would sit together. Both were always open to their own one-on-one connection time as well as joint moments. Just because 'we' expect one to be non-communicative doesn't mean they are – it often means we have to go beyond the *norm* to hear the voice.

In 2018, my family started another journey when we learned that my mom's youngest brother was diagnosed with colon cancer, which later metastasized to his brain. In early March, my mom, my aunt, and I flew out to visit with him. After being on a ventilator, he had a very hard time projecting his voice and therefore spoke very quietly – a rare thing in my mom's family of ten kids.

At one point, a sewer line to his house backed up and it was an all-out effort between several relatives to get the line open to the street. My uncle was a maintenance and handyman for a condominium, and this had occurred many times before at his home as well and he knew what needed to be done. However, due to his voice issues and the fact that he was hooked up to oxygen, he was having trouble getting his point across.

Everyone wanted to take care of it for him – always the plight of the youngest, sick or not – and therefore proceeded to take control of the situation. However, no one saw how agitated he was that one of his strengths was being overlooked. No one, except for me.

I sat as close as I could to him in order to hear him over the chaos in the home, then made others, whether they were inside or outside, look me in the eyes, and listen each time I relayed his instructions. This was the first time in the family environment that I had taken verbal control of a situation; I usually avoided chaos and conflict at all costs as I find it tiring and upsetting on multiple levels. In this situation, however, I knew in my soul that the best way to calm him down was to allow his voice to be heard. I do not know if the others recognized why I was doing it, but the important thing was that he felt heard, and his knowledge was communicated to the appropriate people.

Just two months after this visit, my uncle lost his battle with cancer and my mom and I flew back out for his celebration of life, which, synchronistically, was scheduled on the anniversary of my maternal grandmother's death. During the weekend my aunt and mom wanted to visit the graveyard where she, my grandfather, and one uncle were laid to rest, and once again I found myself traveling with an uncle to a cemetery. Yes, another surreal experience.

Although my dad had to work hard to climb out of the depression and diagnosis from the 2017 incident in the hospital, the course audios that my aunt and uncle supplied him with guided him forward. As he began feeling better, he returned to watching the old shows and news stations more regularly. 2018 and the first half of 2019 was relatively a smooth climb, with the paracentesis sessions setting the rhythm of how life flowed throughout the next eighteen months. It was such a miracle to see him thriving, smiling, and enjoying life after the roller coaster of extreme highs and lows – and a true gift to all of us, both near and from afar, who were walking this path with him.

Twice during 2018 my dad asked if he could be my "overnight pet" when Mom went out of town – a request I happily accepted. I also spent the occasional night when Mom was home so the three of us could enjoy doing our favorite things or just hanging out together. When we were alone Dad asked me to do some Reiki on him; he sometimes had trouble sleeping due to the anxiety he felt in my mom's absence, and Reiki helped. With his science background, he initially did not understand it, but from 2018 forward he would request it more and more, which told me he was beginning to recognize how it benefitted him. Each night as he prepared for bed, I would give him a session complete with music, only leaving once he had fallen asleep. When we talked in the morning, he didn't ever remember me getting off the bed as it provided such comfort and peaceful energy for him.

In the spring another youngster, this one a miniature schnauzer, arrived. He loved *soul connecting* and would gaze deeply into my eyes while enjoying close contact and play together. He had joined the family ten months after another schnauzer kid, whom I'd met during my first year, passed. Anytime I came for a visit, the new pup would continuously bark until I did one special thing, after which he immediately stopped. That one special action was that I acknowledged and greeted his older brother in spirit, who I learned was visiting too.

Afterward, the pup and I had a tradition of greeting each other on the patio: I would sit down, he would crawl into my lap, and we would gaze into each other's eyes. Then the wiggles and squiggles would start, along with cuddles and happy smiles! I would often find him lying in his predecessor's favorite spots around the house, which caused me to pause briefly and acknowledge the other's presence with us.

This kid was different from many I visited at the time in that his stuffed toys stayed intact with the stuffing still inside! In reflection, I wonder whether the situations with the missing stuffing were messages to the family or others about releasing stuck emotions and thoughts that were inside them (*get the stuff out?!*) Sometimes we played our favorite summer game, "toy toss," in the family's long hallway and out of the Arizona sun; other times he would agree to a walk around the neighborhood. Whatever we did – be it connecting in his yard, listening to the nature or birds just beyond the fence line, or playing with his toys indoors – he wanted to be face-to-face with me.

When we did play with his stuffed toys, he would dig in his box of goodies to find the one he wanted to bring to me. His message: *Play is important!* And if we could play side-by-side, face-to-face, or enjoy spurts in the backyard, these were wins in his book.

The same year, I met a middle-aged beagle who was in the process of losing his sight and hearing. His mom was apprehensive because he occasionally fell in the swimming pool, so I always went with him when he wanted to go into the yard to explore or otherwise. I gave him his privacy as he was used to doing things as an independent pup, but I would also stand so he saw me in the shadows of light or felt my energy nearby. This seemed to comfort him, and I knew he understood what I was offering.

When a pet has diminished senses, I have to think outside the box when connecting with them. When one sense is impaired others get stronger, and utilizing games or connection that nurture and build upon those newly heightened ones aids them in moving through the changes as well. This kid's sense of feeling temperature, body sensations, and spatial awareness would increase, helping him identify proximity to people as well as furnishings.

Two months later, I met sister cats who did not find relating with one another a great experience. They truly did not see eye to eye. The more outgoing of the two had suffered a significant loss when a fellow feline passed, and this made forming a connection with the newly arrived, more reserved sister difficult. Indeed, chasing, fights, and power struggles often took place, resulting in one being kept in the master bedroom while the other had the main space as her territory. The door was kept closed between them.

In this household, a lot of change occurred in somewhat a short period of time. Two powerful women moved out, one by crossing over and the other due to memory issues, leaving the two girls with one person to share. When I first began visiting, I would connect with the "main space" girl first, then enter the domain of the other often sitting on the floor while she hid under the bed or beneath a cabinet. As our visits continued, I would put frequency music on, slowly open the door that separated them, then sit on the threshold between them as a bridge to show I was open to connecting with both. I was also acting as a Gatekeeper of sorts.

Over time, they'd go as far as to sit on their adjoining side and periodically do a quick side glance at the other before moving away from the doorway. When their person moved to a new space, the door was kept open between the two. They each still had their separate water, food, and litterbox to call their own. Although they rarely entered each other's space, they would occasionally steal a toy from the other's domain, which I saw as a step up in their willingness to step out of their typical routine.

My next visits with them would prove to show that they were indeed shifting. During my refilling of their food bowls, the more reserved of the two allowed me to pet her as she took a few morsels from the food container I placed on her person's bed. Once again, both sat on either side of me while I did some Reiki after asking if they were open to receive. While doing so, I went from feeling fine to feeling anger arise – and I wondered what had changed. As I tuned in, they were sharing what they were picking up overall in the apartment building from the animal beings, but mostly from the people living there, as a couple moved out of the complex after a disagreement with a newly established rule.

The animals in the building were picking up the frustrations from their people and working to process the energy. While I was there that day, I tuned into the other animals on all four levels of the building, asking once again if they would like to receive then sent Reiki for their highest and greatest good and where each needed it most. After about thirty minutes, the anger within me dissipated.

A day later, they shared with me an image of their mom, along with their questions as to where she had gone. What had happened? I shared with them what I knew to be true about the mom getting sick and having to be moved into a special place that could take care of her needs. I also told them that it wasn't their fault. I then shared this experience with their dad.

In time, another change occurred in the household when the bedroom cat got unexpectedly sick. The dad would find the extrovert cat visiting from afar, but inside the bedroom – for the first time willing to cross the line of previous contention to offer support in the only way she knew how. Shortly afterward, the ill cat crossed the Rainbow Bridge. The other girl and I continued our visits, and she would claim her own chair when her dad had a gathering at his place as she enjoyed being part of the group and festivities. She continues to command a part of the light – and don't forget the t-r-e-a-t-s!

In hindsight, what I learned is that in these pet-to-pet relationships, the challenge often involves one or both parties wanting to be the dominant one; and, when this occurs, one goes through a death of some sort – including a physical death or one being rehomed into a better situation. As I would later learn in a relationship with a friend, this happens with people as well, and often leads to an ending as one or both grow.

Chapter Fifteen

THE POWER OF LOVE

Toward the end of 2018, a senior feline elder came in with a canine brother, who immediately shared his love with me throughout our meet-and-greet. Oftentimes, I would visit with the male feline while his brother went to stay with a canine cousin who lived nearby. The feline was having some health challenges and his parents were preparing both me and themselves for what may come while giving the cat permission to go if it was his time. I was to have one afternoon visit a day with him, providing his favorite wet food, topping off his dry food, refreshing his water, and taking care of his litterbox. The first few days were around the full moon, which often influences some sensitive beings.

During my first visit, I asked him verbally if he would like to listen to some music. Many, especially the elders, enjoyed the various tracks that were twenty-two minutes long. He agreed, and after doing the chores I would sit near him. As I thought about the parents' words about where he may be, I decided to see if he would like me to spend a little more time with him. If these were indeed his last days, I wanted to offer as much companionship and love as I could.

I often had other scheduled pet visits afterward, so I would come early, staying as long as I could in support of him. He seemed a little more alert after the first few days of mainly music and companionship. Most of the animal beings I work with know when I will arrive and leave; in fact, their people, if at home, will report seeing them get up and go to the door a few minutes before I walk in. This particular friend also recognized that I was choosing to stay longer with him. On my part, I always greeted him first.

I would inquire in what order he would like me to do the various tasks for him, offering him the gift of choice. I even brought a favorite deck of oracle cards and asked if he would like me to pull one for him. He agreed and asked for a card, which allowed for additional direct interaction – something he seemed to enjoy. After delivering the card's message I would move on to his food and other duties. One day, after pointing out to him that he wasn't eating much of his dry food, I poured some in my hand and sat close by to see if he would partake – and he did, nearly finishing the remainder in the cup.

He slowly came out of the stage he'd seemed to be in when we met, engaging more each visit in his own loving manner. When the assignment ended, my guides sent me a message that on a certain level he needed to know he was still lovable despite the challenges he was experiencing and the changes in the household animal beings. They also communicated to me that he had been surprised that someone who had not met him before was willing to offer the love and companionship he needed in that moment.

A short time afterward, the family moved to a new home – an experience he wasn't sure he wanted. His parents asked if I could visit him on moving day for a few hours. When I arrived, he was behind the open master bedroom closet door but came out when he felt my energy and heard me speak. He wasn't too sure about the new noises, vibrations caused by the garage door in this two-level house (their previous home was a single level), the new smells, and the noise of things being moved in. In his terms, he was pissed! I told him it was okay to feel his emotions, then offered a new perspective: to see the home as a new forest he could explore at his leisure. Their dog was also having challenges and anxiety as nothing smelled or felt like home. I suggested his dad take him to each room in the house (in essence, give him a tour) telling him that each space was his and his feline brother's, along with the rest of the family's. A few days later, the feline elder was out exploring his new "forest" and they were all acclimating to the new home.

The feline and I had many happy days filled with all his favorite activities throughout the next year. He would surprise me by sharing where my dad was at in his health journey. Often, I would question who he was referring to as I wanted to make sure I was taking care of his needs and where he was, first and foremost, but as I tuned in more to my intuition it became clear. Later, when we were doing two visits a day, there were some definite similarities in their older guy personalities.

One night when I came in for his dinner meal, he said, "Dinner first, greetings afterward!" I laughed so hard at that one! That was a dad thing; if the question was, *Are you hungry?* it was followed by, *What time is it?* – as if to say, if it's a certain time, it's meal time!

The elder crossed the Rainbow Bridge just two-and-a-half months after my own lovable guy – my dad. I learned so much from them both – as well as many of the other pets that I was working with during the months, weeks, and days leading up to my father's transition and afterward. They taught me about the impact of love, the power of interactive face-to-face time and connection, regardless of the activity we engage in; what's important is that each is choosing to do it with one another. Whether the relationship is with a person or animal being, the lessons can be received, understood, learned, and implemented to the best of who we are in the moment, with the understanding we have at the time and the deep love we share.

The feline's sweet and loving canine brother had been working through the addition of a younger canine kid in the last months prior to his contemporary's passing. The two new brothers had very different personalities, energy levels, and ways in which they handled attention of their own and when directed at others. Much of this was the result of the vast age difference between the two, and while having a new young kid join the mix was healing to the humans in the family it created some challenges for the older male, who strived for peace and connection. They both brought their own teachings to the relationship – for the elder, it was the walk of love, while the younger sibling brought the ability to instruct on boundaries

– both his perceptions of them and how to communicate them through action.

Since I see, hear, and understand those typically identified as quiet or silent beings, or those seemingly in the background, I first tend to listen to their actions rather than what they say. The quieter they are, the more I see and hear them. This has come up with mentors as well, whose philosophy is, "Do what I say, not what I do." I will become aware that I have, subconsciously, done the exact opposite; the more I try to *fix or shift to what was said*, the further away I get from that goal. I believe that, in part, this is because it goes against my innate learning style. It is part of the challenge of one who *hears the nonverbal* languages first and really has to concentrate and listen to hear the spoken words.

When I first began doing overnights with them, if I was upstairs the elder would climb up the stairs on his arthritic legs to visit with me. I would work in some love and connection as much as I could without triggering his younger brother's jealousy, which at times was very challenging. When he could no longer do the steps, I would spend as much time as possible with him downstairs, offering love and Reiki.

Less than a year later, the elder would follow his feline brother across the Rainbow Bridge. I visited with him a few days before, sitting on the floor with him and thanking him for all the love and lessons he shared with me. It was difficult to leave that day, knowing it would be the last day when I would see him in his physical form and touch him. As we concluded our visit, this gentleman got up on his challenged legs and walked me to the door one last time. It was so emotional, and even now, as I type these words, tears are flowing from the love we shared – and gratitude for the fact that he still checks in.

The lessons on boundaries continued for much of my early experiences with the youngster. When his people were away, he saw everything in the house as his. When I am at an animal being's house, I want to give them one hundred percent of my time; however, I will occasionally check email or see if any texts have come in – especially during overnights. This kid saw any activity he did not like or didn't involve him as taking away from his time, including me taking a swim in the pool, so he often would react and destroy something as a way to get my attention. Part of this lesson is understanding what they are seeing, creating new boundaries, articulating them to those around us (including animal beings), and shifting our actions accordingly to embody the big-picture lessons they are teaching. I also give myself permission to see my actions and self in a new light and through the eyes of love. With other pet friends, I could pick up a toy to see if they wanted to play or engage in that manner. With this kid, picking up a toy crossed a boundary – it was *his* toy! – so I had to work with him in different ways as he would respond by grabbing something of yours. Ninety percent of the time I'm there he is in some level of teacher mode, so slowing down and looking at his actions overall is key. With an animal being like him, there is a lot of focus energy involved, which, honestly, can be exhausting at times.

Many perceive what I do as a j-o-b, but to me it is an act of love. A business, yes, but one that is heart-based. From our first meet-and-greet to every visit afterward, we are building a relationship of love, respect, and trust. Those friendships don't end with the passing of an animal being, however, they do leave an absence in my heart. I noticed too how the energy and patterns shifted the household. I have seen your animal friends at their saddest (when you first leave), their happiest (when you return), and other experiences in between; however, this one is palatable in a very different way.

What I have learned on this journey is that, just as with our human counterparts, the love doesn't end when an animal transitions! They check in on us in a variety of ways – visiting in the dream state or when we're awake (when we sense them near), an out-of-the-blue saying of their name (by us or someone else), a look-a-like when we are out and about on a walk or at a park, or through a shared memory surfacing. Several have even visited through an animal sibling to show that, yes, they are very much around us and aware of where we are in our own grieving and/or healing journey.

Know they are in your heart now and always. Love is the channel. Put your hand on your heart, focus on his or her face, remember their essence, their character, and feel the love sent from their heart to yours. Always connected, always loved.

These souls know the moment the understanding from their lessons is received, no matter how long it's been since their passing. This is the power of love, and it is the reason no names are included in this book. Yes, each has given approval for our connections to be shared so that you may learn from their teachings; their names, however, I keep close to my heart as a sign of our mutual respect and love. In my experience, animal beings know when someone is speaking of them, be it in person, from another location, or in a book. If someone responds in a negative way or out of anger, the being feels the energy of this, just as a person who you have been thinking about calls the next instant. It is all about the energy connection – the species and distances involved are irrelevant.

Chapter Sixteen

THE CAREGIVER: BEING SEEN
WHERE THEY ARE

*H*alfway through my third year in business, a former colleague contacted me for assistance with her two pups, an elder female chihuahua and a middle-aged male terrier poodle mix. The elder was experiencing signs of aging – including diminished eyesight and hearing, and, later, some canine dementia that caused some further challenges with her finding and using the doggy door. She also began to lose muscle strength, which made it harder to access the outside yard as she couldn't lift herself back up to go in through the door. Despite all of this, she had a happy disposition as she entered her sixteenth year.

Her younger brother had his own difficulties around the changes taking place with his sister. Seeing her have an accident made him nervous; he knew they were supposed to go in the yard and worried that she or both of them would get into trouble. There was a certain anxiety level that increased when the dementia started. And though she wasn't verbalizing in a way humans could understand, she was constantly communicating, which added stress to the situation.

Any time I visited, I let him know he was off duty and that I would take care of her. Just as a person who is a caregiver for a spouse, significant other, parent, or child needs a break (and frequently does not even recognize that it is needed), so too does the sibling animal caregiver. Caring for oneself, whether one is a person or animal being, is integral to caring for others. If we are focused solely on what's happening outside us, rarely are we able to recognize changes – big or small – occurring within us. Often, we hear of the caregiver getting ill or having a lot of health challenges after the one they cared for has passed. Rarely is it that all the things suddenly appeared; it is more that the individual is now not gazing solely outward, and they are seeing and starting to feel their own body as if identifying with it once more. That doesn't mean that we always see the big picture. It is often perceived as something that comes as a result of the other experience, rather than the subconscious choice to ignore our own pain, fatigue, or emotions as there is someone or something we believe is more in need of our help.

For most canine friends, play and connection are integral to living their lives fully. With her going through this change-of-life phase, the activity and way they interacted were also changing, so often he would appear needy to his people. The truth was that he was looking for normalcy and that heart-to-heart connection he had with his sister was slowly diminishing.

During these visits I asked him if he wanted Reiki, and he would race over to me to receive the loving energy. One could see him visibly take a breath as I carried his sister outside, watched over her, and softly verbalized and visualized cues for her as she moved around the yard and patio. Despite the blindness, she seemed to be able to recognize the warmth of being close to someone as well as see shapes in the shadows. He loved her a lot, and she, him. The last visit I had with this female elder, we were outside and when I took a picture of her a rainbow appeared across it. A few weeks later she crossed the Rainbow Bridge.

Afterward, her brother was beside himself as he had never been the only animal in the house since coming to live there. I could see that his struggle was similar to that of a person who had lost their significant other or spouse. All muscle memory with sounds, comfort levels, things occurring outside and inside the home were linked with his sister. Now he was learning everything all over again. Things that did not make him anxious before did so now. I found that after our initial greeting, love, and usually some Reiki, he would lay on or against my lap and nap as it was the one time he wasn't on duty. Now he was the only one on guard, listening to every sound or sighting, which was a brand-new way of living for him.

A person used to sharing responsibilities with their spouse or significant other, must in the next breath shoulder the burdens on their own. It is the same with an animal being that goes from being with a sibling to not. In his case, there was no one to confirm whether it was a normal everyday experience or something unknown.

Although he would lie down when others were not there, rarely did he sleep soundly. This, he shared with me, was because every little sound caused his head to pop up as he worked to discern whether it was friendly or not. I would find this was the case for others who lost an animal sibling and were now flying solo. His house was on the way home from my parents, and one day I wondered how he was doing as his face popped into my mind.

The following week, another change took place. While I was on a networking Zoom one morning, a dove started doing circles toward my sliding glass door, barely missing the window three times. The windchimes also began singing. I recognized the bird's message as something coming full circle and the windchimes were a message often from an animal being. Two minutes later, my phone dinged with a text message from his mom stating that he had just crossed the Rainbow Bridge. He had been sending me his farewell – and letting me know that he was at peace.

At the beginning of 2019, two new friends joined the Dream Pet Care family, bringing with them a multitude of lessons – both emotional and business-oriented. The sweet, sixteen-year-old male pup had started staying by himself more, coming out of his room less, and often was found staring at the walls. His four-year-old sister often needed her space because he had begun following her around e-v-e-r-y-w-h-e-r-e. Sometimes the best we can do for them is to put ourselves in their paws, so to speak, and understand from their personal perspectives what they are experiencing and what they individually require.

I attempted to grasp where each was to support them in the way that was most needed. It was observing what or when the other seemed to become bothered and helping shift the energy of the moment. The sister needed space away from her new-found shadow; he needed to feel the love, connection, and togetherness. He was becoming less sure of his balance and he did not understand that it drove her to the edge.

When I arrived for the first visit, the elder was slow to get moving so I put on some music for him – this, after letting him know I was there by focusing in on his eyes and telling him he could come to the patio door when he was ready to join us. It was very early in the morning when the sister and I went outside for her to take care of business and get some initial one-on-one time with me. After about fifteen minutes, the brother appeared at the door. I softly spoke to them in the pre-dawn light. The sister and I played with her ball while he explored the yard. With each visit, he started joining us more quickly. I served as a buffer for the sister and the brother got the love and connection he needed. During our evening visits, I would offer them Reiki. She loved receiving the hands-on version and would fight to stay awake during it – usually unsuccessfully. Her brother would patrol the inside of the house, periodically stopping to receive and allow me to touch him as he moved through the energy.

Halfway through the assignment, he began playing fetch with his sister and they seemed a little more relaxed around each other – thanks to the combination of one-on-one attention and together play. In the months that followed, shifts were taking place with the elder's mobility. After the sister led him out to the yard area, I would take over, giving him someone to follow and offering cues as he shakily wandered over the uneven rocks. He began following me on his own in between shorter bouts of play or just standing next to me.

Later, he spent more time inside where he was more sure-footed. When he did join us outside, he would often vacillate between wanting to be there and wanting to go back inside where it was safer. It was like he was going through sundowner's syndrome, where the individual gets more anxious and agitated as the darkness comes. It therefore became necessary to split the time between inside and out so the sister could get the movement and play she needed while her brother got the security and love to be who and where he was in each passing moment. We had fourteen days together over a six-month period. He crossed the Rainbow Bridge the same weekend as my dad and his sister crossed over six months later, just before the pandemic.

Just before the younger sister passed, a three-month-old puppy joined their household and was walking through her own set of new experiences. Like many of us, she had to adjust from pre-pandemic life – when she spent time with her new human family and older canine sister, to the lockdown without her sister but the majority of humans home all the time, and then to the reopening, when her people went back to work and for the first time ever she was home alone and in a room with the door shut. In writing this book and reflecting on what I observed in both animal beings and people in 2020 and 2021,

I noticed that both parties exhibited much of the same fears. Some were more fearful or apprehensive about leaving their homes, where they felt some semblance of control; others didn't want to be stuck inside anymore but did not know how to get past fearful emotions and thought patterns.

Indeed, when I met her, the puppy had gone through quite a few changes in her nine months of life. Her first home had a family of felines, and as mentioned, she had come to the present home, her third, at just three months. She had lived there for just five months when her four-year-old canine sister passed. Then, after the lockdown ended, she struggled with being left by herself and would often squeeze herself under a bed not to be put in the laundry area where she slept and was kept while everyone was out.

When I arrived for the meet-and-greet, she was so afraid of me. She would dash in to sniff me and dash out just as quickly. She had a very cat-like way of approaching something or someone new. Big picture: she had never been alone and there weren't any animal siblings that understood her language; therefore, there was no one to confer with about whether sounds, people, or anything else was okay. For the first time, she found herself separated from known people and animal beings to be with a stranger.

It was obvious from my first day of visits that this was going to be a whole new experience for the two of us. She did not want to go back into her room and lodged herself behind a piece of furniture, much like a cat would, and that is where I found her when I arrived during the next visit. She then went outside and would not come back in, so I stayed with her in the backyard throughout the first night to make sure she was safe. The tools I had were love, patience, observation, and a growing intuition. Communication with some previous parents wasn't always well-received, so I would do everything in my power before reaching out to the clients as I always saw it from the perspective of the pet. As I walked the yard, I made sure not to directly face her as this can seem threatening and instead slowly curved my body in a semi-circle pattern away from her one step at a time. With patience and speaking softly, she followed inch by inch from the furthest corner of the yard to meet me on the patio. By 6 a.m., she even played ball. She was fine being inside with me if the door was left open, but as soon as I attempted to close the door she got scared and ran back out. She did not like being in the house by herself. After a quick chat with the family, it was decided we would move her food and water outside while taking it one step at a time.

Over the next ten visits, my focus and intention were about regaining her trust to get her beyond the insecurity that arose with the door situation. I made some progress each visit in getting her back to the center of the yard. I observed that certain noises made her stop in her tracks and jump back or away, and I felt her questions, so I began tuning in to her motions and recognizing what she was becoming aware of while in the yard. I would acknowledge what I was hearing, feeling, or seeing, letting her know that it was okay and what it did in her yard or neighborhood – from the hummingbirds to grackles or quail on the block wall fence, to airplanes or swing sets creaking in a neighboring yard, a delivery truck, or people laughing or walking on the street. I identified every sound I heard and everything I saw or felt in my body. With time, as these things appeared once again, she would look to me and I would confirm what it was by saying to her, "Yes, that's an airplane or hummingbird or whatever," thereby solidifying it in her catalog of known experiences until it became a part of her normal.

She enjoyed receiving Reiki and listening to the frequency music from a distance, initially keeping the yard's pool in between us as a safety net before incrementally making her way closer. I told her how many sunrises remained before her family returned home at the end of each day. I was teaching her that it was okay to be right where she was in this experience as well as giving her space and letting her know I didn't love her any less nor would I stop coming. I would chat softly with her, regardless of where she was in the yard or the process. I also allowed her to come to me in her own time and space, empowering her to make choices based on her own intuition and level of trust. Sharing that touch was a privilege and one that would be her choice as to how we engaged.

During our last few visits, she began lying closer, even going as far as to lay with her back to me to show a huge level of trust had been reached. She followed this by laying three feet away to face me before getting up to move closer to where I sat on the concrete patio floor. She then walked around me as a way to say, *"I am coming around,"* this not as much about the physical action as it was the emotional one. Stopping after the second loop, she laid down on my right side to communicate that trust had been reached and she felt safe with me. With that, for the first time since the first day, I was able to touch and pet her. Near the end of our visit and the assignment, she found her ball and asked me to play with her. Not long after our visits, her family found her a home that could give her what she needed in the form of other beings around and ready access to the outside world, as well as a lot of one-on-one time with her new person.

Chapter Seventeen

BEING SEEN

wo new eight-year-old feline sisters came into my life in early 2019 after they moved to Arizona from another state. I was told I would never see them, so what was I going to do for the hour-long visit? At this point in my business, I only offered sixty-minute visits and overnights; I saw it from the pet's perspective, and for some there had to be a good reason to break out of their normal routine and be seen. I explained to their human that I would offer the felines presence, connection, and time. They would be given the opportunity to choose what they did with the visit, but I would stay for the entire length of time. During the meet and greet, one of the girls stayed out, watching and listening from beneath the table.

When I began the visits, the one sister who had been out during the meet and greet was out when I showed up. I softly spoke, telling her the level of engagement was up to her. I then asked if she would like some music played during my visits with them and she agreed. After I completed the necessary tasks which gave them both time to get accustomed to my energy and presence as I moved about their space, I came back into the main room and sat on the floor to offer them the understanding of meeting them on their terms. With that, I would inquire if she was open to some Reiki and, after receiving acknowledgment from the sister in the room that she was open to receive the distance energy (meaning I did not touch her physically with my hands), I offered it as long as she liked during my visit.

Periodically, she would venture to the food or water bowls to take in nourishment as energy work, like massage, creates movement within the body and many will eat or drink to help with that process.

The other sister would remain hidden until the last day of this first assignment. This more insecure cat zipped around me from behind as I finished the Reiki.

"You do not need to hide or leave," I said aloud, "All interaction is done solely at your discretion. Engagement is up to you."

She stopped in a doorway about ten feet away and watched me for ten minutes; then, after announcing that she was coming over, she brushed up against me and allowed me to pet her for the remainder of our visit together. On the first day of the next assignment and for every visit afterward, she was at the door when I arrived, waiting with her sister just behind her. The sister who was out the entire time previously enjoyed being nearby but did not like touch. The other girl loved to play, to receive touch and both loved the music, companionship, and Reiki.

With time, the family moved to a much larger home. It was during my visit to their new location that their person shared that they were now both coming out when friends were over. Seven months after I first met them, the interactive greeter kitty would come over to check people out and hang out while her more reserved counterpart sat on the nearby staircase to be a part of the conversation on her own terms. Each was learning how to take risks while still honoring what made them who they were, rather than trying to be like anyone else — something we all want for ourselves and the loved ones in our lives.

In March, two new kids came into my business through the Reiki offering. One was going through health challenges and his parents wanted to see if it would help him. He laid up against my legs the whole time while his sister relaxed nearby watching and feeling the music I played during the visit. Afterward, his mom had a session to understand what he might have experienced with the Reiki. The pups continued taking in what was being offered between the two modalities.

A week or so later, I was asked to do some pet visits with the two pups. When I arrived, the ill guy and his sister would ask for the Reiki as soon as I came through the front door. I would sit just inside with the boy lying against my leg and his sister just beyond him both receiving what each needed in the entryway. This was the case for each visit before I fed them, and we enjoyed some time sitting outside together.

After a few weeks, I was asked back to do another Reiki session with him, which I quickly discovered was a mutual gift. While I was out hiking and connecting with nature before my visit, I noticed a family of four ravens sitting in a nearby tree. As they flew off collectively at a point down the road, one split off while the other three continued their flight together. It felt like this was indeed a message about where this family was heading. During my visit with him, I got the distinct impression that he saw this Reiki session as a gift to his sister and parents to help them process what was coming and they saw it as a gift from them to him as it comforted him as he dealt with the side effects of the illness. A week later, he crossed the Rainbow Bridge, and I felt so blessed to have been there to support the final steps of his earthly journey.

One of the messages that came through while writing this book is that sometimes love takes a quick turn-around, meaning a new relationship may only be in our lives for a very short period of time, yet the impact of their love and teachings is huge when it comes to the cycle or circles of life. And, though I didn't see the message at the time, my family and I were about to experience our own version of this scenario.

The animal beings that appear on our path teach us about the importance of love; they also imprint an aspect of themselves on our hearts, regardless of how long or short their stay with us. One of the other things I noticed was that the brother and sister's birthdays were six months apart – and so too are my parents' birthdays. The Universe teaches us that we are not alone in our journey, nor are we walking alone in our pain and the effects of illness on us all.

A month later, I supported his sister as she flew solo for the first time, offering her love and companionship along with some Reiki. As we sat outside on the patio, her brother came through by popping into my mind's eye. I always acknowledge and greet those who join in from spirit. After some one-on-one time with the sister helping her find her way along her new path, a new younger brother joined the family to share her home, and both continue to share love, joy, and happiness with all of the people around them. The youngster enjoys sharing the importance of play in life and seems to find joy in making others laugh.

THE POWER OF JOY

In March 2019, my dad signed up to do a lecture about how the brain remembers things and the difference between short-term and long-term memory from an anatomic perspective. During his career as a chemistry professor, he taught pre-medical students, nurses, and others; now, he was teaching the fellow residents in my parents' community, providing knowledge as well as an opportunity for them to get to know one another and share what their lives before retirement were like. Dad prepared for this as thoroughly as he had when he was teaching his college classes, and it brought him such joy to be reconnecting to his skillset. Indeed, many of the people I have met at my mom's the past few years bring up how much they learned about my dad through his talk that day.

In June, my parents and I had a celebration dinner combining Father's Day with Mom's birthday, which that year fell on the same day. We had such a great time, and it was such a blessing to see him walk in pretty much on his own – happy, smiling, and laughing. These moments were so special – a reminder that every moment is memorable and may hold more meaning depending on where in the journey of life we are standing and what eyes we are seeing life through.

Two months earlier, in April, I had made friends with a mother cat and her two kids; this, after previously giving Reiki to one of the kids, a female who was having some relationship challenges with a sibling when she re-entered the family after a failed adoption. The brother didn't like the attention his sister was receiving from their feline mama, and his refusal to share space was triggering the sister's sacral and root chakra creating trauma in her physical body (specifically her back legs). I realized she did not know what actions to take to rebuild the relationships previously lost when she was adopted, only to then be returned.

During this Reiki session, I opened it up to all who needed assistance in the household, including the two concerned humans. After doing some general energy for the overall space, I offered it to the sister and received a surprise when the very reserved and shy brother came out of his room to connect with me, my hands, and the energy. This move also surprised the people, for this cat typically hid from strangers. This relationship would be revisited in the future after some time away, while the sister's leg challenges eventually reversed and healed.

A few months later, the same people asked me to do a meet and greet with the daughter's three canine kids. There were two senior pups, a female chihuahua, and a male pit bull, as well as a younger male German shepherd. When I met them, their mom was out of the country for several months and the youngster was very anxious about the situation and where his mom was. The female was skittish around new people, and the senior male was a sweet, gentle, and lovable guy. The people were doing their best to check in on the dogs while taking care of their own households and pets. There was also a home remodel occurring during this time, which created additional anxiousness. In later years I would recognize that when emotional changes were not addressed, physical challenges would often appear.

I started coming several times a week, and one of the first things I would do after greeting the crew was offer them some Reiki, which the elders especially loved and would relax into. Then, after taking the younger brother out for a walk, I would play with the trio and offer belly rubs to the elder male – his favorite activity. I gave the sister some time, saying once again engagement was up to her, and, over the course of the first four days, she became more comfortable with touch and closeness. We got into a rhythm, with the three learning to walk together and me learning how to walk with them at their various paces. There were some challenging – and laughable – moments during that process as we often got entangled when one wanted to see or follow a scent in another direction from the others.

I discovered that the youngster loved chasing light reflections, be they from the sun, a flashlight, or some shiny metal object. This was his favorite game, followed closely by playing catch with a ball. His older brother also liked to play with a ball, but his favorite thing was touch. The sister liked connection and companionship. It was important to find ways to give each a little of what they enjoyed most throughout our visits together. When the mom returned, I stayed on for one day a week to provide them with a sense of continuity through this new adjustment. As we ventured into the summer months, we shifted from walks to playing in the yard or inside with toys, along with the Reiki, which was a mainstay.

A few months later, the aunt and her three felines whom I had met during the early Reiki session moved in, which was a new experience for all animal beings involved. They were initially kept in separate areas of the house, and I would do two back-to-back visits, first with the dogs and then with the mama, sister, and brother felines. The siblings still had challenges with their relationship, but now that they were kept in one bedroom they had to make it work. Of the trio, mama was the most outgoing and would play with strings and things with me after I offered them collective Reiki and individual distance Reiki.

With time, the mama feline and the youngster pup started playing "tag" or their own version of hide-and-seek while the sibling cats stayed tucked away in the bedroom, finding camaraderie based on nervousness while still doing their best to stay away from one another. A couple of months later, there was another significant change when the daughter with the younger dog moved out of town, leaving the elder dogs with the aunt and three cats. I shared with the daughter that it was important for her to explain the reason for not taking them with her, as they deserved that respect and sense of closure.

This was a new experience and learning opportunity for the aunt, who'd never had dogs before. Likewise, they were getting to know her and the felines in a new way. The one thing constant for them was the house where they had always lived.

By this time, I was coming once a week. After doing some Reiki with them all at the start of the visit, the aunt would share what had been happening during the week and the response from the dogs – she was looking for guidance as to what it meant and why they responded in the way they had. I noticed that during these sessions the dogs and the mama cat would sit adjacent to me and facing the aunt, as if to make a show of solidarity. I would share what was coming through from the animal beings, as well as what I was intuitively picking up. As the weeks progressed, their relationship started to meld together through love, connection, and understanding as they all truly became one happy pack.

The sibling cats were venturing out into the open space and interacting in new ways with the dogs. Over the next six to nine months, the brother and sister would go as far as to both sit on the bed, with their mama and the aunt nearby learning to find their place and rhythm in this new family.

A new female feline came wandering into my business when her people, who had only left her with family in the past, decided to make a change in her care while they were not home. One of my first experiences with her was an intuitive one via a dream visitation. In the dream, she showed herself seated in the kitchen, which looked as it did in reality – quite rare in dreams. In essence, she was sharing where she would meet me later that morning for our first assignment together. And she knew enough about me to know that I journaled dreams and she was clear enough in the dreams that I understood who was connecting with me. This was the first experience where the pet friends brought pieces of their actual homes as it looked into a dream. And yes, that is where she was when I entered – the heart of the home.

We would quickly develop a routine together that took us in a circle around the house. Greetings, connection, and a chat as I entered and asked how her day and night were, followed by breakfast preparation with her favorite daily selection. In between bouts of Reiki and brushing, she would nourish her body with a few nibbles of food. We then wandered after a bit of play into the living room to listen to a favorite track I found that she enjoyed, and I would eventually begin connecting with her through a modified meditation.

In the beginning, she would go to a resting spot in the house. When I checked in on her, I said aloud that I would be in the other room if she wanted to join me, and from that point forward she would stay out with me. We built a special relationship together filled with love and connection – watching her bird friends out the back door or listening to the ones just beyond her front door, just enjoying one another's company in a state of presence. Then it was onto litterbox cleanup, washing of hands, and a treat before heading out.

As our visits progressed, there were times she would ask that I stay a little longer with her on a particular day. These requests from animal beings are few and far between, so when I receive them I stop and stay as long as needed, even if I do not always know the why. We never know how much time we will have with them. In this girl's case, it was a few more minutes of love and cuddles; other times it was to keep me there long enough to answer an incoming text asking that I stop at a home on my way to my next destination – yes, her connection to the communications all around us were spot-on for her, others, and me.

Other friends ask that I take a little bit longer on a walk, play a few more minutes of music, spend more time sitting in connection with them or gazing at the yard at night. Believe me when I say they know what is coming from an energy standpoint, yet they may not understand what it will mean exactly for them, their people, or me – but they feel the change in energy coming. And, as it comes closer, they begin responding and their behavior often does shift. Some spend less time out in a main room, sleeping more, or wanting more time to interact with you. One pup started sleeping more or would be sleeping when I arrived when one of her people was counting down the days to retirement – the pup had heard and sensed discussions around their next steps that would take us away from one another. Just as they will miss seeing me and our routine, I too will miss the love, connection, and laughter with them; for, after all, we have built a friendship around acceptance, understanding, and forms of similar communication with one another.

This sweet feline would do this as we moved into the pandemic and scheduled events kept shifting. When we reconnected in 2021, nine months later, she had developed diabetes, which is often connected emotionally to a deficiency in connecting to the sweetness of life and in response to the heightened anxieties, challenges, and shifts taking place. I was blessed to be able to support her on the level that I could through our favorite activities, music, and the love we had for one another while a vet tech took care of the injections and testing.

Later, we would walk through more change together as she was acting less like herself – laying underneath a table instead of her favorite place atop it and then spending lots of time in the one room I had never seen her in, which was the coldest, darkest, and most inner room in the house. After speaking with her people and the vet tech, I spent additional one-on-one time with her in the room she found herself in for as long as possible, offering extra love, Reiki, music, and support. A short one month later she crossed the Rainbow Bridge, exactly nine months from when we reconnected in 2021.

In March of 2023, she came in through spirit for a visit accompanied by the sounds of the music she and I always listened to together. It was one of those wonderful signifiers letting me know who was coming through from the spirit world, as she was the only one for whom I played that particular music. I shared her presence with her people. She came in three days in a row, during which time I sat listening and meditating with her to the hour-long track. These were special moments, and she brought through the message, *Play the music and I will be there to help you sink in deeper. You do not need to do everything alone, we understand you. You are one of us, always have been, and always will be. There is not anything you could do that will change our love for you. You reminded us that there are those out there that see us, regardless of how much of ourselves we perceive we must hide in the darkness of time and space.*

This message of unconditional love and acceptance carried a depth of emotion I have rarely experienced and surely will never forget.

There are those who look, hear, and touch but don't see, listen, and feel what is beneath the surface. And, yes, there are some who spend years and even lifetimes learning how to discern whose emotions, pain, and thoughts they are actually feeling in their bodies. The best analogy I can offer is that of identical twins, where one breaks a leg and both feel the pain as their own. The one who has *not* broken their leg must then dig deeper to understand whether the pain is an illusion or their truth. It is often a matter of acquiring the tools through knowledge and observations, then applying those learnings in the moment. It can feel akin to inventing something that has not ever been seen before; there is no how-to video for the way one distinguishes how you feel different in your body than another does, or how to separate yourself and your emotions from that of another person, being, or environment around you. It is no surprise, then, that your first steps have you engaging less, keeping several feet away, and detaching to not absorb *this time*. It reminds me of the separation scene in the movie *E. T.* – because I had always connected in that manner, I did not know how to be in close proximity and in relationships with people without feeling and treating everything as my own.

When it felt like my fuel tank was empty after an hour of being around someone and I felt like I was fighting to stay awake even after doing a lot of grounding, shielding, and personal inner work, I began asking myself if the relationships were healthy for me. The bigger question that surfaced was whether the relationship I had with myself was healthy. Was I nourishing myself with foods and beverages that supported me? I thought I was, based on what was perceived as healthy in mainstream media, but was I truly nurturing myself enough by doing the things that gave me a sense of presence and connection with my body, mind, and soul? Again, I thought so, but quickly realized that I had to give to my soul the things she enjoyed with sheer inner happiness; then, when space existed in the calendar, I could choose to do something with another. Like everything else, I figured out who I could hike with and who I couldn't depending on what I strived to achieve and made sure that the activities that fed my soul the most did not get removed due to someone else's wishes. This was a trial-and-error process that led me to stand strong in my truth: hiking is non-negotiable – my prescription for staying in alignment and that which shields me from imbalances in my energy that, if ignored, eventually lead to discord, illness, and pain within my body. If I have learned anything from those with whom I have walked through medical situations, we do not want to uplevel an imbalance. Likewise, I do not need to understand another's choices for I do not want to walk their health experience to comprehend their decision firsthand.

Was there an imbalance playing out between how I was caring for myself inside versus how I was caring for others…with the quantity and better yet was the energy and care I provided to myself not of the same quality? When I could feel my dad's pacemaker as if it was under my skin and the times throughout the years since that feeling showed up, I have had to ask myself, *What do I need to do for me? What healing do I need to do? What changes do I need to make? What do I need to release to not walk in the footsteps of my dad's health journey to eliminate that lesson from showing up in my life?*

Chapter Eighteen

THE LOOK OF RESPECT

A new family of feline kids arrived a few months later. I have come to recognize that when I have a lot of visits with mainly cat families in a row, the lessons focus on connecting within, meditation, and doing some more intuitive exercises. Yes, I am there to assist your animal kids, but there are also symbiotic teachings they just offer by being exactly who they are. As the felines came into my world, I would also be learning new ways to communicate as this family consisted of a higher percentage of feral cats, reserved domestics, and a few extroverted felines who often acted as gatekeepers for those younger or more insecure. These guardians were an older mama kitty who provided a safety net, an aunt of sorts who continuously moved any of the Reiki around taking it to the hiders in the group while connecting with me in her own way, and a middle-aged big brother who was a lovable character.

When I entered their domain, I would always sit down just inside the doorway to connect in their own preferred manner with those who were open to do so while finding that window of presence. After a few moments, I asked if they would like some Reiki and those who did would pile into the room or lay across the thresholds between the rooms. Mainly the gatekeepers came the closest before others would come a little closer sniffing my hands, feeling the energy, and being ever watchful and curious. I shared with this group as I had with many others, engagement is up to them. Many feral cats have more insecurities passed down from their mamas, as well as due to their own experiences, so I generally gave them the space to choose accordingly. Learning through observation of how I was with the others, as well as hearing and seeing their sibling's responses, slowly led them to widen the door to me and what I offered.

In a few months, I would also introduce the frequency music and was pleasantly surprised to see some of the more insecure ones make an appearance. Different musical tones establish opportunities for new connections. As they responded and became at ease with these, I brought some different colored shoelaces that further bridged the gap, as a long shoestring gave them another security net beyond their gatekeeper siblings. Watching the guardians play and have fun was key, especially for the more reserved members of the group and those who had never experienced this type of *play* in their external street world...they didn't always understand the concept.

Not too long ago, a mama feral delivered babies in the yard and my client brought them inside, eventually getting the mama and, when they were of age, the kittens spayed, neutered, and checked over. Since it was wintertime, the family was kept in a separate room indoors. When I began visiting with them, I would start by solely addressing the mama – after all, if a stranger wanted to connect with my kids, I would want them to go through me first too. Love and respect are key to the success of building new relationships regardless of the type of being.

Mama lay atop a dresser, ever watchful of the door, while her kids remained hidden behind a table. I asked Mom if she would like some Reiki and she blinked, which in my world means yes. I sat on the floor while softly focusing my gaze upon her and did some with her, taking it one step at a time. She slowly relaxed her body. The next visit, I offered her some music with it, again addressing just her. With time, I brought the shoelaces in, and, after doing some Reiki and playing the music, I showed the shoelaces to her and asked if it would be okay to share them with her kids to see if any wanted to play. She acknowledged my question while continuing to watch over me. One of the female kittens displayed the most fearlessness; she would play with the laces then slowly engage a brother to play with us as well. They liked having the ability to choose up close or at a distance. Mama and I always chatted first while doing the Reiki, and with time she would go as far as to face away from me and take a nap, understanding that I wasn't there to hurt but to love and empower them. With time, the other two kids also came out, at first tentatively and then more boldly following in their siblings' footsteps. Since then, their mama has chosen to go back outside while her kittens chose to remain in. They see one another from afar as Mama and her brother hang out in the yard, quite often enjoying the secondary food, fresh water, and beds that are provided. Others who visit are humanely trapped, taken in for spaying or neutering, checked over, and then released or taken to a no-kill shelter to find a family of their own, depending on their own willingness to connect with two-legged beings.

In the four years I have known them, the majority allow touch or some connection in one way or another. For a few it remains from afar, but I understand; it is about accepting them as they are. The kittens, on the other hand, have grown up and love playtime, cuddles, and touch.

Chapter Nineteen

A WALK OF LOVE

On July 15, my dad once more landed in the hospital where he was diagnosed with atrial fibrillation (AFib); following this stay, he began going through another cycle of falling. He went on an experimental prescription drug as most of the typically prescribed medicines he could not take due to other health issues. When my dad began falling, it told us that something was shifting once again in his body as he also gained fluid more quickly in his abdomen requiring more frequent trips to have the paracentesis procedure done. This was the tell that we didn't want to see.

A week later, messages of another type started coming through which told me we were on another path. One day, as my mom walked me out to my car after visiting with them, she stopped to pick up her mail and found only one item: a newsletter from hospice. As I was driving home, a funeral procession came toward me on the two-lane road, and, the following day, a package "mistakenly" delivered to me that was of hospice supplies. This was where we were heading. We did not know the timetable, but the destination was clear. There were times when all I could do was shake my head as the synchronicities lined up once more, and do my best to breathe through the current experience, trying to stay present rather than worrying about what the future held for us.

Between this time and August additional shifts were occurring as well. Dad began telling me stories I had never heard before – specifically those about growing up around his grandmother, who spoke only Italian, and how he loved doing things with her. He also started wondering what his Uncle Tony (who had died in the war before Dad was born) was like, which made me think Tony may be one of those in spirit who would be picking him up or guiding him forward. On my way home, I inquired what this uncle was like and was shown a character from a tv show we all watched – a vision I shared with Dad. He also shared the childhood memories of his uncles, including adventures they took him on and how they looked after him when he was bullied by kids at school. One would make him lunch at his nearby shop.

On the flip side of these happy discussions, Dad was more tired and could no longer understand how to work his electric toothbrush or razor. During this time, I was having a variety of messages coming through the dream state, as well as lyrics from songs such as Bob Hope's "Thanks for the Memories," which held so many meaningful insights. Many of these came through at times when my dad was taking early morning naps, which led to questions of whether I was receiving from him or other relatives already in spirit.

A few nights later, my Jack Russell friend brought through messages around my dad's decreased mobility. I awoke one morning and found I could not move my legs; this, after having dreams of Dad's legs being stuck in a stone wall and of a car with its bumper and back tires flat. I quickly realized that my legs couldn't move because my buddy, for the first time ever, was lying on my legs – much of animal beings' communication comes via what they typically do *not* do, and this was one of those times. As for the dreams, walls often represented something blocked or veiled by Spirit, which is how I read this message. Cars in dreams can be another representation of the body – in this case the flat tires correlating to a person's legs that are not working. All of this, in addition to the song *High Hopes for a Living* coming through regularly, was a reminder to keep our focus and mindset in a higher place for my dad's journey – and to see the big picture.

Going through something like this has one thinking about life in general, and I was no different as I finalized a process to be initiated if something unexpected happened to me. It laid out the steps my brother would need to take with regard to my business, including the notification of clients. There seemed to be a lot going on, sometimes too much to process while things were occurring.

Toward the end of August, I returned from a short trip to visit my brother and sister-in-law to find Dad's condition had deteriorated even quicker than expected. One thing I had learned along the way is that the timing of how things unfold is out of our hands, and this was no different. The day before my parents' fifty-fifth wedding anniversary, I visited with them for the first time after my trip away. Just a few days after this celebration, my mom asked for my help because she was struggling to assist him in getting from one room to the next, to the bathroom, and through his anxiety.

For the next month, I would use their place as home base from which I ran my business. I spent every night there, and, as much as possible, I arranged my pet companion visits so I could help during the day. My dad would call upon me to assist him as he believed I could do anything physically to aid him, as well as talk him through the anxious moments and keep him safe. Within two days of my getting there, things shifted in a big way: my dad went from being able to stand for a short time before needing his walker to the communication between his brain and legs completely deteriorating. It was a very emotional situation as individually and together we tried to navigate this vastly changing landscape playing out before us. At this stage it was almost impossible to move him, even with the help of my mom and despite his being a smaller man. Dad could no longer help with the movement of his body; it would simply go limp, and we had no choice but to rely on a wheelchair to assist with his mobility.

All of the animal friends I visited with during this month were sharing messages in one form or another. As my relationships with the three dogs (the chihuahua, pit bull and the German shepherd) deepened, they began sharing where my dad was in his health journey in a variety of ways, such as using their positioning in proximity to gates or doors to explain while offering me support as I walked through the experience. There were cycles of not knowing what I was feeling, but being able to share this aspect with these special beings helped me move through this process in a whole new way. The sister cats would do this by getting my attention purposefully, crossing over a threshold between the hallway and one of the bedrooms, and gazing up at a light to share that he was heading from the physical plane to that of spirit as he went toward the light. Hallways often represented passageways between dimensions, planes of existence, or realms – as in Dad traveling toward someplace else.

My dad's last appointment with his cardiologist was a challenging one for several reasons. He inquired if there were any other options available to help on his medical journey of the heart and was told no – everything that was known, trial or not, was exhausted. At this point Dad asked the doctor to write a directive that he go to hospice – my mom could no longer take care of him at home. Although this was a true statement, it is never easy to hear this with a loved one. Part of it is understanding just how far we were able to travel with him on his journey at home before the situation was taken out of our control. We were all lost in our own thoughts on the way home.

A day later, he was moved to hospice care and of course found himself staying on the same floor as my maternal grandmother had seven years prior. It was surreal to be there again; indeed, as we walked through the place, the emotions and observations of the past situation with my grandmother seemed to surface for reconciling in our hearts – from the floor with its familiar and yet disconcerting feel and the restaurant, to riding the elevator and entering his room, where everything was a shade of brown. For me and Mom, it seemed dismal, which I think was amplified due to where we were at in his journey and what we were recalling from our previous walk.

A week later we had another drop-in-our-stomachs moment when during a procedure Dad's pulse plummeted and the hospital staff did not think he would come out of it. I had multiple visits with animal friends that day and it was only at the last moment that I decided to go for the procedure. I was able to stay for two hours before having to leave, and I did my best to connect in with my dad via my heart/intuition silently, saying how much I loved traveling with him through our life experiences together, how much I learned, and how much I loved him. I also shared that if it was his time, and I wasn't meant to be there today, I would understand. Otherwise, I would be back in three hours. My mom and I knew that my brother and his family were on the road driving in, and I shared that with my dad. It was *very* challenging to walk out of there not knowing what was about to transpire, but as a solopreneur in my business I had others who needed my care that day. The hospital staff did not understand my decision in that moment, which made it more challenging, yet I knew I had to put my trust and faith in the higher powers, and in my dad, in that moment.

As I was writing this, my dad brought through a memory of a road trip he and I took together. We were eating egg salad sandwiches along the way, and the egg salad was squeezing out through our fingers and down the steering wheel. And, just as we had in the car that day, we laughed together. It was a reminder to find the lightness, love, and lessons in each experience.

After my visits, I took a deep breath and called my mom to see what was going on. She told me Dad was back in his room in hospice –shortly after I left his pulse started returning to normal – and that the hospital staff could not believe his recovery. My mom and I felt strongly that Dad got the message about my brother and his family traveling in to see him. One thing my dad didn't like was feeling he was missing out on family time, and, in this case, the party planned for my nephew's sixteenth birthday.

The following day, we had the party with food from an Italian restaurant we loved and an ice cream cake roll with mint chocolate chip ice cream, which was another family favorite and held special childhood memories for my dad. With help, Dad was able to eat his favorite spaghetti and meatball dinner, enjoy some of the cake, and sing *Happy Birthday* to my nephew. He rose to the occasion. A few days later, my brother and family would head back home, and my mom and I would enter the next stage of our journey with Dad.

A dream message had come through exactly one month prior to the birthday showing that loved ones in spirit would be getting together for an Italian dinner at a restaurant. At the time of us having the gathering I did not recall the dream – that came through during a review months later, as was the case with many other dream messages (I was bringing through between five and ten a night, as well as in other ways.) This particular dream I did not recognize until writing this book.

My mom and I spent every moment we could with Dad. For me, it was in between pet visits. The two feline brothers would offer me a gift in September as well as beyond. With these two there was a special connection, and perhaps it was that trust we built over the first several years together that opened this new, special doorway for communication regarding my dad.

As Dad began sleeping more and speaking less – this started on the evening of the 16th – the more reserved of the two boys began showing up in unusual places in the home as well as acting differently. It took me a while to recognize that this gentle soul was opening a door through which my dad was interacting with me. Prior to this it often felt like my dad had trouble understanding why I'd shifted from working with people at colleges to working with the animal beings – and this was an opportunity for him to experience me and my work in a whole new way. Likewise, his feline brother began sharing where family members in spirit were gathering – in a *family room* of sorts – and at what point things were shifting.

There was a dichotomy now, for my dad was no longer opening his eyes yet we knew he was still hearing us on some other level, and doing whatever work he needed to in preparation to transition. I would then visit the felines and share this new experience with my dad while at the same time receiving messages in many additional ways via songs played on the radio. Every time I got into my car two songs in particular played: *I've had the Time of My Life* and *Shallow,* with the latter talking about his ascension from the physical to spirit.

Wild beings, mainly in the form of hawks, showed up all around me and Mom as we traveled to and from my dad's room, which symbolized him watching over us wherever we went and the importance of the big picture. I also saw other signs while out and about on my travels. These were coming through more frequently, along with the ongoing dream state messages from those in spirit. In addition, I was recognizing that dream messages that didn't feel like mine were coming in as my dad was traversing between the states of consciousness in the days leading up to his transition.

My mom and I did a lot of processing of our observations, emotions, and whatever else surfaced in our evenings after leaving the care center. We were doing our best to take care of nourishing our bodies, getting some sleep, and rejuvenating ourselves throughout the day in between staying with Dad. Something we had learned during earlier hospital visits is that, in order to support him, we had to maintain our own health and keep up our energy levels.

There were conversations and movie-style dreams, where he showed himself to me as a young boy, lost and looking for his mom and dad in a building. I took him by the hand to guide him to where I knew his parents to be. In another dream, I saw that his number, which came in the form of a license plate, was called to spirit, and that three family members would pick him up. I also saw that he was given his exit strategy, with his and other names showing up on a chalkboard – which seemed fitting as Dad was a professor and administrator for much of his career.

In yet another dream, I was led into a hidden or sacred movie theater space with angel sentinels guarding each corner. My dad and his father sat on the left side of the room watching the people in the audience, who had played some type of role in my dad's life, as the review of his earth life played on the movie screen. During this, I sat next to Archangel Uriel (on his right side), watching and noticing that periodically my mom went up to the front row to take care of my dad in some way before returning to sit next to me.

The feline brothers began to show some movement with regard to my dad's journey home, and where the family members who were going to pick him up were. Dad was moving from being in the "living room" (the physical space of those living amongst us) to walking along the "hallway" (a passageway to another realm of existence) and eventually being close to connecting with his parents in spirit (in the feline brothers' home, the one showed himself just outside the master bedroom). My mom and brother also shared the messages they were getting around Dad's journey at this time.

For me, there was so much coming through, and in a variety of ways, that it was hard to keep up with all the meanings and truly understand every reference. At times I would get a name that had no meaning for me and had to ask Mom. In one such case, the name Emerson came through as someone supporting my dad in some way. I learned in talking with my mom that this was the name of a man who lived in my mom's hometown when she was growing up; he would occasionally invite her parents and the ten kids to his home for a meal. He was sending a message that he was helping my dad too.

While out driving around on my way back from some visits, alongside one of the roads was a red pickup with the words
"Caretaker" on the back of it. This, of course, had a greater
meaning to me, as well as the fact that there were more red
vehicles, which to me represented family in spirit, surrounding
me than ever before. More understanding came as my mom
and I sat with Dad, holding a vigil with him, watching over
and talking to him, and just being present with the experience.

Afterward, I was getting messages that my dad was in
training for a bicycle race. During one of the practice runs
it was raining, which often represents a cleansing or renewal
cycle. There was also a guy landing on a boogie board atop a
snowy mountain to guide another man (my dad) down the
hillside to family and friends awaiting his arrival. The dream
messages and those occurring during the waking hours started
to meld together; for example, that of a person rubbing my
dad's back appearing in my early morning recollection and
later walking into my dad's room to find my mom rubbing
lotion on his back. What I did not always recognize at the
time was that the timelines between my night visions and
life were merging. We were entering a whole new cycle, one
where pictures were being taken and used at an event in the
dreams, which is something I would create afterward for my
dad's celebration of life.

Some of the most profound messages involved people,
who had played key and supporting roles in Dad's lifetime,
returning to their home in spirit where they changed out of
their "costumes" – or roles they played in support of dad's
journey home. After they changed, they went into a room

with other family members and friends to celebrate the success of the journey.

During a visit with the chihuahua, pit bull, and German shepherd before he moved, the lyrics to *Rainbow Connection* began playing in my mind. The youngster, the g.s., who had been lying on my lap, got down and kept his eyes on me as he walked from the living room beyond a gate and into the kitchen. My dad was beginning his journey once again from the land of the living to the gateway and onto the heart – the spiritual and Divine home of pure love.

On the 20th of September, we honestly were not sure whether he would stay with us. It was my maternal grandmother's birthday, and given their past relationship and experiences with following one another, we did a lot of deep breathing as we moved through the moments of the day. This was a difficult day to leave for any type of nourishment; we pushed ourselves to do so, but it was challenging, nonetheless. In addition to the messages coming through the music, dreams, life, and the animal beings, I was also receiving them through angel numbers. One morning, I awoke at 4:44 and was guided to look at the clock at 4:56, and 5:00. The message was that angels and loved ones were all around, and Dad was taking the necessary steps to continue forward on his path. He was moving through the last phase of his "physical therapy" on the upper levels and going through the light to a "medical office" for spiritual healing, shown as a door identified with a number seven.

Chapter Twenty

THE LAST CLIMB

New experiences started happening as I felt my dad's emotions as he headed toward a new dawn, a new beginning. The path forward to honor someone's wishes is not an easy one, but it is *their wish, their choice, and their path* that we walk with great respect. In the days that followed that would become even clearer through the messages and experiences brought forth. *In the middle of the night, I found myself seated at a table within a circle of people and I am holding a blueish green chrysocolla crystal necklace, the stone of a master teacher which allows one to speak the deep-seated wisdom held within. While I am sitting there, a raven card is pulled with the message of rebirth/death of the self, and I am being told I cannot stay any longer in this physical world. With this declaration I feel left out as I run from the room.* As I connected with my dad in the dream state and went to him after seeing this experience occur for him, I made sure he knew that he will *always* be part of our family even when he is on the other side – he is always welcome to hang out with us.

As we entered the morning of the twenty-second, a dream message showed a large group of athletes running to the top of a very high staircase where they received an award. In the background of the dream, the theme music from *Rocky* played. The award is that of completion of their journey along their earth path. Another message depicted me seated in the backseat of a car with my dad driving and my mom in the passenger seat. I ask my dad if he will be okay, and he says yes as he lets me out at the top of a circular road. After grabbing something from the trunk of the car, I begin walking down the road. As I watch him continuing to drive, he drops my mom off a little further down before coming back around to watch me walk my path.

As I drove to the home of my feline friends for the last visit of our assignment together, I stopped to pick up the mail and I was guided to do a loop of the subdivision, which is unusual. As I did so, from a path on the right side I saw a young boy on a bicycle riding along it and after I moved beyond the spot, he crossed over, and I knew I was meant to be where I was that morning. Yes, the little boy, my dad, was on his bicycle making his way home. This was transpiring the way he wanted it to be – and if I could do anything for him, I could honor his wishes and dreams for all of us. When I walked into my client's home, one of the crystal-like clear glass stones or something similar that sat in a bowl on a shelf in the living room was lying on the floor and cast rainbows all around the room. My dad's mom and other family members were on the ground to lead him home.

I was at the restaurant with my friend when I received the call from my mom. I took a moment to collect and steady myself before driving over – and, yes, to eat the sandwich that just arrived moments before. Anyone who knew Dad would find this appropriate – the one thing he always asked during any of the hospital emergency room experiences was when he could get a sandwich or some other type of food. Now, he was making sure I got food in my system before the next stage, as well as imparting some humor as it was a well-known family joke (*"Mangia, mangia* – eat, eat up!"*).

On my way to his hospice room, I stopped to get coffee for me and Mom while we waited for the University of Arizona medical school to come pick up my dad. He had donated his body to science to teach one last lecture. There was a hawk out traveling with me to the hospice center, reminding me to see everything from a much higher perspective, see the big picture and focus on the moments of love, joy, and laughter that filled our days among the hiccups and challenges. After the person arrived six hours later to take Dad for his "final class," the song "Somewhere Over the Rainbow" came through. Mom and I worked through the immediate process of collecting my dad's things from the room, moving the items into her van, and driving back to their place.

The quiet in their home seemed deafening. My heart didn't know what to feel. My mom and I tended to be doers, so when we walked in it felt like the never-ending task list had been ripped from our hands and, with it, all understanding. Everything took on new meanings: my dad's place at the kitchen island, his office, his coffee cup, and the place he last sat in the room as we watched a light-hearted, happy-ending movie. In his last months at home, he wanted more light movie and television selections. Those who have walked the path of grief know you see through new eyes and a new heart as everything feels and looks different, somewhat empty and absent of the love that filled it only precious moments ago.

My dad and loved ones in spirit were very much with us, from his last physical moment to his first spirit-bound moment, as evidenced by continuous messages and signs. Dad also helped us maneuver through the paperwork and every step since then. My mom and I had a massage scheduled from the month before a few days afterward, which felt important to keep as it helped us begin the process of working through the emotions, thoughts, and physical experiences that we had in the days and weeks before. It also shifted our perspective from being focused outward to taking care of ourselves and our bodies. While in my session, I received word through a visual image that my dad was teaching his last class for a group of medical students. It was a very surreal moment and experience.

He found ways to show us he was around and assisting us. One such situation was to get us to a sit-down restaurant, get in, out, and to our appointment an hour later without feeling rushed at noon time on a Friday. He and others continue to make their presence known. Whether it is the song *Blue Moon, Come Fly with Me, Sway,* or any other of his favorites, he shows us every day in some way that he is walking the path with us supporting our journeys whether together or separate, and how much he loves us. Much of the information that came through would be deciphered afterward in a review of all the messages and signs six months after his transition.

CELEBRATE THE JOURNEY

A week after my dad passed, the German shepherd, pit bull, and chihuahua I had begun watching in early 2019 opened themselves up to share a message from him and his parents – first in a dream visitation showing my dad in a backyard with a blue collared shirt and my grandparents coming out to the patio. The next day, while out playing ball, the youngster started gently and playfully pulling on my shirt and when I asked why he was doing this, the two senior pups came out onto the patio standing in the exact location as my grandparents had in the dream – and the youngster had a blue collar! Yes, my dad was coming through the youngster to play with me, and it was a message that the three were together again. It was such a wonderful gift! I so appreciated their ability to share a message like that at that time and in this manner. It was so needed, and the message was clear – find ways to play now more than ever – celebrate the love, the journey together, and the joy!

Two months later we had my dad's celebration of life. I was visiting with the eight-year-old sister cats that weekend. The girls made sure I wasn't left alone the whole time I visited with them. If one wanted to go downstairs to eat, she waited until her sister arrived and sat adjacent to me; this was the same when they switched, always making sure I had someone with me. Yes, they understood the need for support.

Chapter Twenty-One

LEARNING TO HEAR
MY OWN VOICE

*T*here have been lots of understanding and messages surfacing through the process of writing this book that gave me a much higher view of my early beginnings. Being a quieter kid opened a door to allow my other senses to heighten – specifically, the ability to hear, sense, and feel those I perceived as quieter than me. Throughout this journey, it has often been the animal and nature beings, as well as people, like those depicted within these pages, and messengers of Spirit.

A world-level deep dive into some of the base-level emotions took place in 2020-2021, when as a whole we were asked to do tasks and everyday things in new ways. My mom and I took this to heart, doing a lot of hiking in nature in the weeks and months following my dad's transition as the movement assisted us in processing the emotions, memories, and loss while doing something we both enjoyed (ironically, being in nature was something my dad did not enjoy). Surrounding ourselves in nature, hearing the songs of birds, the gentle breeze brushing against our faces, and the warmth of the sun touching and soothing our shoulders, allowed us to integrate our individual and joint understandings along with releasing and being with grief in a new way.

We also discovered that doing old things in new ways helped us move through the constant memories of Dad's absence in the physical and feel into the spiritual awareness of his presence and support. We did everything differently, from where we stayed overnight, where we ate, and the way we drove on a road trip to my brother's home after the reopening following the lockdown. We still walked through the memories recalling times of laughter, sadness, and joy of road trips out Interstate 40, but we were not faced in every moment of the trip with our missing muscle memory link, my dad. Instead, we were able to celebrate the new path and find joy in some of the new opportunities.

A favorite adventure memory that guided us toward happier times was when my sister-in-law was pregnant in 2003 and my parents and I decided to take a chance to drive out to surprise them and, hopefully, be there for the birth. So we jumped in the car on a whim (or early intuitive nudge) for the ten-and-a-half-hour trip and headed toward Texas. We were beside ourselves that we would miss a call or not get a message as much of Interstate 40 had no cell phone service between Winslow, Arizona, and Albuquerque, New Mexico as well as parts of the east side of Albuquerque on the way to Amarillo. While seated in a restaurant the morning of September 12, we received the call that my sister-in-law was in labor. With a happy cheer, we quickly finished our meal and raced out to the car. Now thoughts switched to hoping we would get there in time.

We were in a more elevated vibe as we prayed we would make it – which we did with a few hours to spare! We were all there, and my nephew officially had his first "committee" (people and pets included) – which is what we called ourselves whenever we stood or sat in a circle around him. As I am writing this, I recall that in his toddler years my nephew used to love, and nearly demand, that we sit in a broad or narrow circle around him with everyone in the same room. Sixteen years later we were all together again on my nephew's birthday, a circle of love once again. Yes, Divine timing and his own willpower at work.

By year two of the pandemic it had become increasingly difficult to maintain a connection within as I felt I was being bombarded by opinions, perceptions, and the like. Previously I had been able to stay out of the fray; now it felt like regardless of where one stood we were being pushed more in various directions to see whether we would hold our own, bend to someone else's will, or crumble under the force. Whether in general, by friends, or by family – beliefs and judgments were flying in all ways. In 2021, the wall and point of no return was reached, whether a byproduct of grief or in combination with all the external noise. When conversations became more draining than energizing, I had to take a closer look at what and who I was to stay in close contact as my energy levels were constantly shifting.

It may have been the footsteps through that eighteen-month period that began sinking in as to the ways one needed to focus on one's own health and what was key to healing oneself in the process or what may be detrimental. Within weeks, several relationships went through a pressure cooker process with most being centered around similar themes. It got to be I just could not go through it one more time. We have all heard the phrase, *the straw that broke the camel's back,* well that one relationship I spoke about in the beginning was the last one of its kind.

It kind of felt like Spirit was saying, *At what point will you say enough is enough and stand up for you and your health? At what stage will you see this particular relationship isn't working or healthy as it stands for you right now? At what level are you going to allow your personal vehicle – your body to be heard, seen, and listen to its voice? There may not be a tomorrow, or I could end up repeating the lessons of that relationship again with another person or another type of relationship.*

One would think that standing up for yourself or your health is easy, but for someone who had put themselves last on the list if on it at all since her earliest memory of existence, it was extremely challenging.

The walk with the animal beings has taught me the importance of self-care, communication, acknowledging my feelings or emotions, and shaking off what doesn't serve me in some way on my path forward. They have been teaching me to accept myself for who I am and where I am, throw the rulebook out to start again – and acknowledge the love and lessons each has brought to me and allow them to flow where they are meant to in the moment. Forgive myself with grace for the steps I felt I needed to take, forgive others for not being who or where I needed them to be in order to keep moving together with them, and thank them for being the catalyst to help me move to a deeper level of understanding of what steps I needed to take in my own healing journey. There were also things I learned I had to dig beneath the surface into the hidden emotions, pain, and patterns to fully integrate and embody to release the lessons once and for all.

This relationship was critical to making that leap, to gain footing in the depths of the unknown, and to take the inspired actions my body and soul knew I needed to take toward my health. There was an ongoing thread to go within and listen.

On this journey of healing and wholeness, there has been a need to step back to see the truth in experiences and relationships through new eyes – both those when my role was understood and those where it seemed vague. When I did this, I saw the opportunities and additional doors that were available yet not in my level of awareness at the time. This brings me to the question, was I always meant to receive this higher level of insight at this stage? I believe the answer to be yes. Every step and choice brought me to writing, comprehending, and healing in this moment, and without the challenging relationships, situations, and lessons, I wouldn't have been able to break through the layers of illusions to see, feel, and speak my truth. I had to walk through the difficult and uncomfortable emotions, the experiences to find my path out of the darkness, and the silence to move forward in bringing my understandings into the light. As my guides have been sharing, it is time to shatter the glass and break through the wall to a whole new version of myself.

During the past two years, I have been hearing *and*, more importantly, *listening* to the whispers of love from my soul guiding me to the *classes, inner work,* and stretching myself to look at each choice through new eyes. To do the deep dive into the soul and the perceived wins and losses into a life review of sorts. A walk through the perspectives of perceptions, truths, and illusions to discover a new me that had been hiding deep behind the silence. Sitting in the darkness of the protective shield of needing to feel safe and the only way to stay safe was to remain silent and not allow myself to act by perceiving it as not time. In recent years, I have heard and seen this question a lot – and it seems more pertinent now than ever – *If not now, when?*

Chapter Twenty-Two

PUTTING THE PUZZLE PIECES TOGETHER

*I*n 2022, just before the holidays, several pet friends in spirit or those in different living situations came through with messages for their families. Some, by seeing an animal friend that looked just like them, others by jumping up and down behind a block wall fence so I could just see their face, and others watching me walk another dog with a message for her parent that even as she walks with a new pup friend, her pup-in-spirit is watching over them. Other times, it is a feline in my mind's eye that shows up sitting on my right shoulder as I am driving – and still others come in to walk another loved one, human or pet, the last steps to the Rainbow Bridge.

The year before, I began to first question the car accident in 1989 and started to realize that the energy of the impact had to go somewhere. Intuitively, a memory from a networking meeting presentation came up as a possible opportunity to learn whether anything else was associated with the presence of the tremor. Further questions surfaced as to whether communication or expressing myself in some manner was part of the connection and the resulting shaking was a plea to be heard or seen.

On March 8, I began to recognize that I was like many of the animals that came into my life – although I found it difficult to verbalize into words, my other senses were coming online and learning to take center stage. I was learning to hear and see what others often did not, as well as feel what was happening inside for others. I was learning that I was a wide-open vessel that did not always understand shields or energetic self-protection techniques. Instead, I felt and experienced other beings' "stuff" – emotions, thoughts, or physical aches and pains – believing they were my own.

This was an aspect of the teachings that would not be understood until the last two years, when I began to disengage from the things, situations, and relationships that were no longer healthy for me, including the one within myself that told me I needed to keep myself small in order to fit in or remain in the status quo to live out others' perceptions of who I am to be. I realized that was no longer who *I* wanted to be and that the teachings provided through my relationships and the love discovered with the animal beings, loved ones, my dad, and with myself through this process were now meeting up with the Divine Timing to reach forward and open the long-awaited door.

Viewing the steps and the emotions of the past as words coming together on a page gives us a higher perspective – one in which we can see ourselves and the movement from the space of strength, what we faced and overcame, the journey from the silence and observing the outer world to witnessing the inner world's progression. Learning the language of the soul, and putting a voice to the feelings. It was learning to separate myself from the energy, physical sensations, thoughts, and emotions of others with the ongoing forward pull bringing me to the present moment.

Often, we do not believe we are doing enough to move ourselves through the layers of our journey. Seeing my actions on the page opened a doorway into what my own dedication and hard work looked like and the ways in which I faced that which appeared. I saw how I maneuvered through the stories of my youth to reach the lessons and love within. I was able to take myself by the hand to come out of the background learning about myself, new ways to communicate, and head toward being with the present moment – and the peace I was seeking.

Fast forward to learning how to start communicating in new ways when I turned nineteen, a time that, as previously mentioned, involved a number of beginnings and endings. In essence, I was learning silent systems such as customer relationship management software programs and solidifying the knowledge through re-keying the data over and over which allowed me to absorb the information into my memory in ways that hearing spoken knowledge did not. This method of repetitive learning taught me the cities and zip codes within Georgia. This was followed by being cross-trained in a hands-on or applied learning process on the five key components of managing an accounts receivable process. Each piece was handled by a different coworker. This resulted in a strong foundation from the ground up that led to me handling the entire donation process. The pieces of receiving the donation, understanding its source or where it came from, keying the data into the software, sending an acknowledgment letter, depositing the monies, and reporting back out of the system. I did this process daily which is how I still, thirty-five years later, recall specific number codes for entering the information. This is a form of communication, though not everyone has the aptitude or affinity for it just as not everyone is a highly verbal communicator. This doesn't mean one person or way of communicating is better or more brilliant than the other. These silent-type computer programs use printers to access the inner data, much like that of the human body's brain. I always wanted a printer to download information from my brain. Now I understand that it is finding ways to access my voice, which is not solely a verbal process, as how one writes or feels is also a style of expressing the knowledge.

What is healing? It is often seen as a destination; however, like many other paths it is the journey to happiness. It is finding what we are passionate about, what we love, and what gets us out of bed in the morning. What is it? Healing is every step, every moment we are present in life following our joy and living life to the fullest.

Our journey of healing is not only about us but also about the patterns we are clearing from the ancestors who passed before us. As mentioned earlier, one of the patterns I discovered during my healing hikes was that of the *strong, silent types* that did not know how to find their voice, did not know how to break the silence and unlock the door to release the information and emotions held deeply within. Sharing with others wasn't always received well by some people, nor was finding an opening. It can be like attempting to get a word in when speaking with a salesperson on the phone. For me, it is like negotiating with a bulldozer; it doesn't work. Some conversations with strong verbal people feel the same way, as we have completely opposite styles of communication.

What I have discovered with time is that often the latter are not at ease with sitting in silence, so it is difficult for space in the conversation to become available while the more observing non-verbal or quiet people struggle with finding an opening. As a result, it becomes a one-person show, with the other person feeling constantly unheard or unworthy. Many of these relationships become more toxic than healthy – both with others and myself. It became like information overload as an abundance of words, thoughts, and emotions were held within the sound of silence. When enough of this occurs within the body, it is like waiting for a computer system crash, with the only options being to uplevel the memory card or exit the program and find a healthier way to exist.

When it came to this pattern, my predecessors achieved as much as they could; then it was passed to me, most likely before I was born into this life as it seemed to start at a very young age. Through the years, I was challenged to find the window of opportunity while learning to interpret the feelings and non-verbal communication into words to be on an equal playing field. This has been a fifty-four-year journey of healing through each step, each choice, each yes or no in connection with myself. I am learning what decisions feel authentic to my body and those that feel out of alignment with who I am. I understand that when we feel as though we are walking an unknown path we are actually on the journey of recreating and healing ourselves to truly follow our soul's distinct compass, release the old, and open ourselves to a new way of being.

By bringing this shadow into the light to fully accept and integrate that truth, I was able to heal the old belief around it – both for me and my ancestral line. The walk with the animal beings has opened the door of reflection to see them and myself as one, to see us as whole, and to see us as integral contributors of what is often hidden beneath the surface of silence, to walk together in peace and discover the next chapter in the journey.

Every ancestor within my family line who has lived this pattern of not understanding how to release their voice to be heard, to be witnessed as a valuable member of life, felt this integration. Their celebration with me came through loud and clear when the words from the first stanza of "Amazing Grace" came through, releasing all to be seen clearly while that which was lost was found through the whispers of love, compassion and, finally, through self-acceptance.

In seeing my path forward through the many distinct layers of growth, I started to understand the journey – from the unawakened being, into the chaos, the pathway to stillness, and the unknown with possibilities of all kinds. Now, I have become awakened to see the puzzle in the moment, as pieces that need to be identified, joy to be felt, happiness to be lived, understanding to be mastered, and lessons to be learned in order for the next cycle to begin.

Rarely do we open our eyes wide enough or really feel into and through the resistance that arises as we get to the space of feeling misunderstood by others. Really, the one we most want to be understood by, the one we want to believe and trust, is the one within us, as that is where our truth, love, and all the answers for our unique journey are.

Stepping out of the details or emotions brings a greater level of awareness, understanding, and the ability to fully integrate the teachings that have been occurring since day one of my life on Earth as follows: I have been learning about signs, being a guide, navigating life and the road ahead, being a bridge and/or translator of the silent, quiet and not understood by all. Feeling deeply that which was mine and, mostly, what was not, which I held deeply inside, not to be revealed or heard even by me.

By 2011, I had experienced twenty-four deaths of beloved relatives, friends, and colleagues. That year brought another passing, this time of a colleague in another department who I respected greatly and felt seen, heard, and accepted by. This loss was so challenging, and another that was so untimely and unexpected. Each experience of grief was unique and handled very differently. And my losses were not always actual deaths; there were also forty-five people who left the two college departments where I worked, most of whom had left for other opportunities that also affected me to various degrees. Rarely do we see people again once they have left our daily environment.

I found myself reluctant to welcome in new relationships easily, as I feared getting attached only to have them leave, which, to me, mirrored death. I struggled with the vast array of emotions brought about by these experiences and I became invisible in many ways as a protective mechanism of my heart.

It was in 2012 that I began opening the door a bit to strangers via writing and sending packages to deployed military personnel in a variety of circumstances. This broke through a wall in my heart and allowed my creativity to flow as I packed unique boxes filled with goodies, uplifting cards, and letters. For a little over a year, being of service to them lit me up in ways that my work no longer did. Then things shifted for me and I went through another series of losses: selling and downsizing my house, losing my job, grieving my maternal grandmother, facing the end of a dating relation-ship, and coming to the realization that I could no longer do the type of work I was doing or be that person anymore – all within a nine-month period.

The fall of 2013 was about embarking on a new journey to find who I was and who I was meant to become while work-ing through the process of grieving all I had lost. A year later, my dad had his heart attack, which led us on a new path while I worked to identify this new and evolving me. The door was opening to the practice of being me in the public eye at fairs and networking events while being of support to my parents through Dad's early post-heart attack hurdles.

November of 2015 brought an intuitive shift into focus, challenging me to recreate myself and work through the parallels going from hidden to visible, silent to relearning to communicate, and from behind the scenes to being on the stage of life. This was the beginning of my working less with systems and working more with the unknown or the silent messages of the soul. This led to the new focus of animal friends in 2016, which would help me grow, teach me about self-love, unconditional love, and walk me through expanding more to different styles of communication – all while learning to be an interpreter of other "silent" languages and beings and building relationships with many human clients as well.

By the time 2019 came in, I had experienced the deaths of another close relative, a family friend, and twenty-two animal friends. At this point, life was very different; I was receiving messages via the dream state, numbers, and a variety of other ways – this would be heightened in the months to come. This year was also my most consistent year in business, when, despite all the challenges, I was busy from the end of June to the beginning of November. Several experiences with the *father* figures within two client relationships brought about major changes. Unbeknownst to me, these were messages of things to come. One retiring at the end of June which brought an assignment to a conclusion, and another in early September where the husband was in an accident that led to a decline in movement. Both of these would bring greater understanding to how additional messages from spirit were coming through with regard to my dad.

That year, we saw my dad reach his highest point since the heart attack – in February developing a class on the brain's capacity for short-term versus long-term memory from a chemist's viewpoint of an atom, and on Father's Day walking into a restaurant assisted only by a cane. Only a few months later, however, he sunk to his lowest point, when he no longer understood how electrical devices worked and his legs were unable to receive commands from his brain, followed by his transition from the physical body to spirit.

After my dad's transition on the 22nd of September, Spirit kept me moving forward in my business, with the most pet visits since it began, while I continued taking steps to stay in the space of seeing life from a much higher perspective.

Seeing, experiencing, and receiving information in these ways took me on a very different style of grieving as I knew he was around me, from the moments leading up to his last breath on this side of life to seeing him once again in dreams when he was on the other side. He and others in spirit guided me six months later to type up all the messages that came through from the middle of June to his celebration of life in November. And still, my dad is always connecting...and I am sure he *always* will be.

What I learned in the days and weeks to follow was that self-care was critical. In order to move through this new experience, I had to find new ways to care for myself and my body while integrating what I had learned from Spirit to change how I grieved, processed, and walked a new path of understanding when it came to death.

Chapter Twenty-Three

INTEGRATING AND EMBODYING
THE TEACHINGS

*A*fter eighteen months of listening to the countless perceptions of others on both sides of the aisle, I had to listen to my body's need for peace. What I found was listening to anything else for too long was draining for me. I began tuning in and taking notice as to how long it was before the exhaustion set in and conversation tired me. In the beginning I could do it for three hours, however, this dwindled to less than an hour during that year and a half. This wasn't living life and thriving.

I felt like I was surrounded by everyone's version (known and unknown people) and I was searching for the higher perspective. I knew from the higher vantage point that some of what I was seeing was the pendulum swing of the previous cycles that worked to unsettle one side, only to then do the same chaotic movement through the other. This recalibrated everyone's point of balance to a new level.

It seemed like the more I searched for a way to tap into peace, the more those outside wanted to bring in their own version of chaos. Once again, I found myself precariously balancing on the surfboard of life. There were times I could maintain that sense of being within the flip-flop of conversations and others when there was nothing tangible to grasp. When that became the focal point of every conversation with every person, I began seeking more time in nature as a way to refuel myself, which I found clearing, healing, and reinvigorating. This was especially so while still working through and processing my grief that surfaced for release as the experiences began to thaw that once seemed frozen in time while our focus was purely on the pandemic.

With every conversation bringing the depletion more to the forefront, I had to be more discerning as to when, where, who, and how long I could stay around the energy. There was so much push and pull going on that I was struggling with whether I was meant to stay in certain relationships. Even when I voiced an opinion or searched for a level of peace, common ground, or truce, I was met with very little.

I would ask for a change in venue or location with some of these relationships, hoping this would shift the topics, but it did not. Finding what I could ingest on all levels beyond food and beverage was key. That which was occurring in the mainstream wasn't it. When every get-together became more of the same with an increasingly draining effect, I knew I was going to have to begin lessening my time spent with this relationship.

I tried just backing off and allowing some space, however, the other party kept attempting to hold on more. It came to a head in the latter part of 2021, when I recognized that the relationship simply wasn't healthy for me. This was one of the most challenging decisions I'd ever made, especially since until that moment I didn't recognize that there could be non-dating relationships with such unhealthy or toxic attributes. (This type of thing had happened before when a dating relationship took control forcibly past no). Now I was learning that, regardless of the nature of a relationship, one could feel as though they continuously had to hide aspects of themselves or be who or what another wanted them to be. In this case, it was no longer solely about boundaries or an imbalance in the way one related to the other. I do recognize that there were times in this relationship when I mistook my lack of stating my needs as holding space for the other. I have learned that often there is a fine line with this, especially when you are one that has rarely spoken as you searched to maintain the peace.

The decision to step away brought with it more back and forth, mimicking the previous outward push and pull within myself. I checked within myself as to whether I was doing the right thing, as this was the first time I was standing up in support of my body. I was coming face to face with every statement and belief that in the past told me there was a way to work through every situation, hold onto the relationship, or focus on supporting the other person. It was only through deeper analysis that I realized that, had I stayed, I would have allowed my own self to further diminish and keep me in hiding even from myself.

As Spirit guided me to various classes and books, I began going into nature more to work through the questions, what I needed to learn about myself, and what I had not seen previously. I have been diligently listening, loving, forgiving, processing, releasing, accepting, and embodying long-forgotten aspects of myself, as well as the parts not ever recognized to get on the other side one step at a time. And there are still moments that arise from the ego aspect to question the choice in connection that walks hand in hand with my soul, who is looking out for my best and helping me see what I have not. I have worked through karmic family lessons and others, all while in the healing surrounds of nature – hiking, journaling, meditating, and doing voice recordings to move energy and understandings from the inner to outer world and then refilling my soul. Each hike is an opportunity for processing what surfaces, either for acceptance and embodiment or change and releasing the old to bring in a new way to be.

It is understanding and recognizing the early lessons that showed up in the packages of love and humor to test an unrealized agenda while also being in a space to see the points of *uncomfortable* in others that moves them into an out-of-character role. Some of it is understanding the difference in perspective between what is seen and what is felt, depending on what side of the relationship experience we are on, what side of the teaching we are on, and whether the words spoken are the truth of what we felt, saw, and heard from the actions of the other, versus the action or non-action of myself.

I have wondered whether it was solely this life, or many, or some karmic family line of lessons, patterns that has played out to teach me whether someone will be there to catch me if I fall or something will always jump out of the dark at me. Whatever the case, the higher, bigger picture of these early lessons was that I should not be too comfortable in my skin or any environment, as that is always shifting and changing. That I need to feel into who I can trust with my heart, or who truly has my back and will step in to help if asked. It also taught me that it was important to be completely self-sufficient, as that is what I strived to be in every situation and that I needed to continuously test myself to stand on my own two feet (that was part of the move from Georgia to Arizona). I learned that I could honor my own counsel, regardless of how scary the unknown was.

This began shifting as early as 2014, as I opened the door more with my mom without going into the details of my walk to discover my new self. I began sharing more as we walked with my dad on his journey, assisting one another, and some others. After 2019, we learned new channels for supporting and communicating.

Chapter Twenty-Four

THE WALK OF HEALING

The path of healing after a loss, whether that of a person or an animal, involves similar stages of grieving, processing, walking through the absence, dealing with the missing link in their life, and experiencing familiar sounds that now seem different. Often changes in sleep patterns can occur and the feeling of the lack of being with someone who understands them in all the same ways. One may not have someone else in the house to ask, "Did you hear that sound? is it normal?" It becomes a very quiet surrounding, whether for the human or animal being. Whether we hear something externally or not does not mean no communication is occurring; whether we see a human or animal being with no tears does not mean they are not crying or that there is no emotion; and whether we see his or her eyes closed does not mean they are sleeping soundly; nor does less apparent moping or joy in the weeks or months following mean they are ready for a new companion or to be in the house alone.

The struggles of a caregiver and the relearning of self-care within an ever-changing dynamic made me see life in a whole new way. This experience within the parallels of dramatic highs and lows had me digging into the pieces of my foundation on a personal level, as well as from a business perspective. This time was to refocus on self-love and learning to ride the waves between gratitude and struggle, from grieving to seeing the light in situations, and centering my focus on me and Mom learning to walk again without the third side to our triangle.

During the lockdown phase in Arizona the one thing we were permitted to do was be in nature. This began a journey of grief processing, when we would discuss what we were experiencing to release, remember, and move through it. There were circumstances unique to each of us, as well as memories and experiences held together. The varying situations of that time had me facing each day as a brand-new event with all aspects shifting in some way. Mom and I found some open drive-thrus where we could get breakfast and coffee after a hike, having a picnic of sorts in our vehicle while continuing to connect and process the emotions associated with grief, as well as the ever-changing landscape.

2022 revealed another layer of grieving as the lens began shifting from the pandemic walk to a new way of living and with that our eyes shifted to situations and experiences closer to home and new memories of my dad that were surfacing. As a family we spoke of how we were feeling the emotions in a different way than we had the previous two-year cycle.

Things would once again surface in a different relationship; this time, however, I recognized, as the result of all my focused healing work, that I had to find a way through or find myself back in the same space with a new person. When I began opening myself to a higher perspective, I quickly learned that I would be asked to see experiences with very new eyes from every direction to understand why it was appearing before me and on what level I was needing resolution. This is why the relationship of 2021 was so pressurized, "over the top," and different from where it began; why what brought us together was blown into a million different pieces and other directions, so we were no longer growing in the way or along even similar paths as we once had.

There would be tests by the Universe to see in what situations I honored myself, and still those that tripped me up… and these would often show up whenever I felt a level of guilt at taking care of myself instead of accepting more business. It was a test of what was more important, helping another, or taking care of my body. Part of my journey of healing came to a head quite literally when my body, with the Universe's assistance, upped the ante. As I have shared, I had experiences with teeth that took years to work through, overcome, and heal. In December of 2022, a few days before Christmas I received a wakeup call that I thought I could handle while being of help to another in a dire situation. The Universe and my body called bullsh*t to that while at the same time heightening the lesson – an infection at the base of a root canal and a reaction to local anesthesia triggered increasing and constant tremors, as well as swelling from my jaw up to the middle of my forehead while decreasing the ability to open my mouth to less than a quarter-inch. It was just enough to get a straw in to eat and drink, and even that small movement was laced with pain.

There were things I tried that worked and there were those that didn't. There was a lot of learning and finding gratitude in the small steps forward over the three weeks. I am very grateful for blenders, my family, the urgent care places that were open on Christmas Eve, and for the hotel that was willing to aid us in finding a vehicle to get me to the urgent care if needed. Let's talk about the lesson: one needs their mouth, jaw, the muscles in the side of the head/face not only to eat, drink, brush your teeth, take medications, but also to speak up for oneself – and I had to admit how painful it was, despite not wanting to bring that type of attention to myself, be a nuisance to others, or wreck holiday plans. It was very challenging, as I was not able to hold a cup as my hands shook so bad that at times someone had to hold my cup or bowl and the straw for me.

Yet, I still went on the trip, flew on airplanes, and visited with family. This too felt like a lesson from the pandemic that if you could be around family, do so as connection was important. All of this is a vast reminder that it is key we stand up for our body, our intuition, our spirit, and our heart or face the consequences of the body increasing the volume on the dial. The other lesson for me in this experience was to not feel like everything was shifting due to me as one typically does not want to be the cause that triggers changes during the holiday season. It was not only about learning to ask for and accept help regardless of whether it was Christmas Eve or any other time. And though we think we can mask or hide our pain, it often makes it more visible.

For me, teeth were all about getting to the root of a situation. I became an investigator of sorts, working to uncover the clues to guide me forward to what was at the core. And the core is love. The teachings began with loving myself enough to speak up and stand up for me; loving myself and my body enough to walk away; loving myself enough to follow my intuition in every situation; loving myself enough to listen to my body's cry for help, whether on a holiday or out of town or if I needed help to be able to eat or drink; loving myself enough to receive the support and care offered whether from the animal or human beings; loving myself enough to refill my body's tank, not necessarily with food, but with joy, play, and love – and learning to do so daily.

Identifying the experiences that constitute those energies is key when I have been so focused on creating a successful business while recognizing the focus must be on love, happiness, and joy. I know it is the harmony that truly creates a successful business, a healthy me, and a legacy of love. Loving myself enough to honor my body's connection to nature, and submersing myself in its energy each day, is what creates that balance.

I am learning to trust what is arising and believe in myself and my intuitive ideas, as well as guidance from angels, the Universe, and loved ones in spirit, including my dad, to help keep me moving forward. I am discovering that every time I get a nudge from my intuition and take the step to communicate, express, or write something, I am healing myself from the inside out; it is in those moments that I am rewriting the book of me. I am learning that when I find uncharacteristic emotions that go against my strive for peace, I need to feel into the why, take myself into nature and the present moment to understand its origin, then embody and accept that aspect of myself that has at times laid dormant inside or where the source has been hidden.

Without the strong base of love, respect, and teachings from the animal beings, as well as the incremental progression of standing up for my beliefs and early understanding of what I was observing, hearing, feeling, and deeply knowing along with the walk beside my dad, I would not have recognized the need to truly listen to my heart and body as to what was working or not. It was in walking the journey beside them through love, loss, and heartache to finding a way to traverse the pathway to healing via self-love or quite literally die trying to stay in what no longer worked.

The animal beings' faith in me, the lessons they lovingly provided, and the journey we walked together were some of the most loving and challenging of the heart. This has been very much a soul walk, offering a glance into worlds beyond this one. These beings and others share with me a continuous thread of guidance and support during my Soul's journey home, with whispers of love guiding me every step of the way.

THE END.

CONTINUE THE JOURNEY

*T*hank you for reading my book and opening your heart to the opportunities, teachings, and love that can be found in relationships with animal beings. Living the life situations, relationships, emotions, and understanding more about myself were a journey on their own. Writing this book was yet another adventure – and a deeply surprising one that allowed me greater insight into the big picture.

My hope is that through witnessing my steps you have learned more about yourself and the path you are walking. So much more is often occurring than we see in the moment.

If you feel inspired to follow me on my journey:

- **Download my new e-book, *Fun Activities to Enhance Connection with Your Pets* when you join my email list at** www.kellyvizzini.com/blog **to receive my weekly blog,** learn about my business, animal connections, new services, and updates on where life is guiding me.

- **For your animal beings that struggle with separation anxiety when you travel,** check out my newest service the Remote 3-Day Animal Reiki Travel Package. Reiki is sent to your pet(s) three days in a row in support of their emotional needs starting the day before you leave, the day you leave, and the first full day of your absence. A daily intuitive writeup is emailed to you of what came through each session. Learn more: www.kellyvizzini.com/shop/p/remote-3-day-animal-reiki-travel-package

- Contact me via my website at www.kellyvizzini.com

ABOUT THE AUTHOR

*K*elly Renee Vizzini is a Reiki Master, Animal Reiki practitioner, and author of *Are You Picking Up Your Messages?* which was published in 2014 and available on Kindle. She is also the founder of Dream Pet Care LLC, which focuses on love and respect to gain trust and build symbiotic relationships with the animal beings in her care by offering them the rare choice of choosing the level of engagement from day one.

Kelly brings together Reiki, sound therapy through music, intuitive communication, and pet companionship, which she offers in forty-five-minute or hourly sessions as well as overnight visits where they are most at ease – in their homes in the northwest Phoenix area. She also offers Remote Animal Reiki services, sending energy to animal beings who struggle with separation anxiety while their humans are traveling.

Kelly Renee Vizzini resides in Glendale, Arizona where most days you can find her out hiking in nature, connecting with the animals, seeing life through the lens of her camera, and enjoying life with her family. Kelly also loves new adventures, whether she finds them in the pages of a light mystery or on travels with her mom around the globe.